No
Easy
Game

By Charles Paul Conn

TERRY BRADSHAW
With
CHARLES PAUL CONN

NO EASY GAME

FLEMING H. REVELL COMPANY
OLD TAPPAN, NEW JERSEY

The publishers are grateful to the Pittsburgh Steelers Sports, Inc. for providing many of the photographs in this book.

Library of Congress Cataloging in Publication Data

Bradshaw, Terry.
    No easy game.

    1. Bradshaw, Terry. 2. Football. I. Conn,
Charles Paul. II. Title.
GV939.B68A36   796.33'2'0924   73-11270
ISBN 0-8007-0623-4

TO
my lovely wife
MISSY
who, since she entered my life, has made
every part of it richer and more meaningful.

Contents

No
Easy
Game

1
Miracle of Pittsburgh

IT WAS ONE OF those fantastic, impossible plays that you don't believe—even when you've seen it with your own eyes!

It was a miracle, as surely as David killed Goliath and Jehovah delivered the Hebrew children from the fiery furnace!

It couldn't have happened. And if it happened, it couldn't have happened to *me*, Terry Bradshaw. But it did happen. It happened in front of eighty football players, fifty-five thousand live witnesses, and ten million people watching at home on TV. They all saw it happen but me. I missed the whole thing because I was lying flat on my back at the time, with two guys weighing a total of 530 pounds sitting on top of me.

What it was, was football. Professional football.

The Pittsburgh Steelers were the good guys on this particular day. We were a scrappy bunch of ballplayers who had been kicked around the National Football League for forty years—and suddenly—in 1972—had erupted. We had won eleven games and lost three, and claimed the first division championship in Pittsburgh history. Our fans had gone crazy at the sudden arrival of success after all those years of famine. And now they were jammed into Three Rivers Stadium to see their heroes beat the Oakland Raiders in the first round of the pro-football playoffs.

Only it wasn't working out that way. At first it had. At first everything had gone just as they wanted—the Steelers had gained a lead and held it until the last desperate moments of the game. But then the roof caved in. It happened abruptly. Oakland quarterback Kenny Stabler was forced out of his pocket of pass blockers, scrambled to his left, and suddenly sailed forty yards into the end zone to put the Steelers behind 7–6 with less than a minute on the clock.

Now the only hope was for the Pittsburgh offense to do the impossible—move the ball the length of the field in less than a minute on that tough Raider defense. The man on the spot was *me,* number 12, quarterback for the Steelers. And all I could think as I watched the specialty teams line up for the kickoff was *I can't believe it—we just can't lose like this after coming this far.*

When I trotted out onto the field, I had four plays to do something. So I started. First-down pass—incomplete. Second-down pass—incomplete. Third-down pass—incomplete. That left one play, and 70 yards to cover, with Oakland defenders spread over the field like a quilt.

I took the ball from center, dropped into the pocket, and was rushed hard by two linemen. I scrambled to my right, turned, and ducked just in time to evade a tackler, stumbled back to the left, saw Frenchy Fuqua upfield, and cut the ball loose. Then I got creamed by two Raiders and sprawled flat on my back, wondering what happened to the ball.

And that's when I heard the most ear-shattering roar that ever came out of the throats of a football crowd since the game began. The stadium practically trembled with the noise, and it rolled on and on, a long, passionate, sustained roar. I didn't know what happened, but I knew that somehow the Pittsburgh Steelers—like the Hebrew children—had been delivered!

The ball had found its mark upfield, had hit Fuqua and free safety Jack Tatum simultaneously, popped free, and been picked out of the air just above the turf by Pittsburgh back Franco Harris, who ran unscathed into the end zone for the miracle touchdown that won the game for the good guys. That was us—the Pittsburgh Steelers.

The next day I was flat on my back again, only this time I wasn't draped in sweaty linemen, but in the clean white sheets of a hospital bed. That wouldn't have been so bad, I suppose, if I had been there with a rough-tough football injury, a badge of battle like a separated shoulder or a broken nose. But it was nothing so glamorous as that.

I had diarrhea—intestinal flu—call it what you like. All I know is that I had the biggest game of my career coming up —a game for which the Super Bowl was the prize, the AFC championship game against the Miami Dolphins—and I was so sick I didn't even care.

The bug hit me the night after the Miracle of Pittsburgh, and I stayed in the hospital all week. I was so sick I didn't sleep at all for two nights, lost sixteen pounds, and had my insides probed with a glass tube the day before the game to check the possibility of a ruptured colon. I got a little better by the day of the game and went straight from the hospital to the locker room at Three Rivers Stadium to do battle with the team that had won fifteen straight games.

At kickoff time it was 77 degrees in Pittsburgh. I went through a brief warmup drill, threw a few passes to loosen up, and walked to the bench so exhausted I could barely stand up. I was drained, sick, woozy. When the game started we moved the ball well, marched it right down field, right to the Dolphins' doorstep. From inside the 10-yard line I took the snap from center, rolled to my left, and sprinted for the end zone. I just made it, just barely stretched into the corner of the end zone when the lights went out. I got cracked so hard I couldn't get up, and they had to lead me off the field. I don't remember very much after that, except that I kept fading in and out for the rest of the afternoon. My head began to clear a few hours later—after we had lost the game and the season was over and the sun had begun to go down.

That's football. It can take you all the way up and all the way down within the space of a week. It has room for all the highs and lows a fellow could want in a lifetime—and I've had a pretty good chunk of both come my way.

2
How It All Started

MY FOOTBALL CAREER started with all the promise of a busted play.

Looking back on those childhood years, there's no doubt about it: I just wasn't very good. I have read biographies of professional athletes that tell about unbroken success from Pee Wee League on up. You know the type: they start by breaking all the kiddie league records, are named All-City in junior high, All-State in high school, and All-American in college, leading their teams to fame, glory, and perfect seasons along the way. They get to the pros never knowing what it feels like to be cut from the team, or even to sit on the bench. There are lots of guys like that in professional sports —but you can bet your bottom dollar I'm not one of them.

The first time I remember playing football was in the second grade in Shreveport, Louisiana. There was a 75-pound Pop Warner League in the community where I lived, and I played on a team in the second grade. I don't remember much—only that I was small and skinny and played guard on the offensive line. I got the stew beat out of me every day —and loved every minute of it.

The next year my dad was transferred from Shreveport to the little town of Camanche, Iowa. Camanche was a nice enough town, but it wasn't exactly the hotspot of the sports world. There was no kiddie-league football program at all, and my football career came to a sudden halt. For the next several years there was nothing to play but baseball. I became a pitcher on a team in the Camanche Little League, did pretty well, and enjoyed it. But football it wasn't, and all through those years in Camanche I pitched baseball and dreamed about football.

I think what I missed most was the roughness—the contact—of football. I loved contact as a skinny second grader, and I still do. I like to hit and get hit—and also like to *avoid* getting hit sometimes, depending on who the other guy is! But that's what I missed most about football—that feeling of rough-and-tumble contact that baseball just can't provide.

In the absence of a team to play on, I played alone. My older brother Gary didn't enjoy it as much as I did, so most afternoons I played in the backyard by myself, throwing the football at whatever target was most convenient. I threw the ball at tires, threw it at buckets, tore down a swing throwing it. I threw it up over the clothesline, caught it, and dodged imaginary tacklers. I was passer, receiver, and running back all rolled into one. And it sounds childish and cornball, but right out there in that backyard in Camanche I decided I wanted to be a professional football player. I was pitching well enough in baseball that I knew I had a pretty good arm, so I threw that football in the backyard and dreamed about the day when I would be a pro quarterback.

There was one big problem with that ambition: I wasn't any good. My family moved back to Shreveport when I was in the seventh grade, and I counted the days until I would enter Linwood Junior High School and try out for the football team. Finally my chance came.

It was the first week of school, and I was sitting with my buddies in an early morning class when someone came around from the athletic office to read an announcement. It was short and sweet and to the point: WILL ALL BOYS INTERESTED IN PLAYING ON THE LINWOOD WILDCAT FOOTBALL TEAM REPORT TO THE SOUTH BLEACHERS IN THE GYM AT 3:00 P.M. The announcement touched off a shock wave in the back of that classroom. We poured from the room when the bell rang, with visions of gridiron glory running wild.

"Hey, I wanna be quarterback!"

"Yeah, I think I'll be a wide receiver."

"Hey, I'm gonna play defense!"

We were all so excited we barely made it through the day.

When 3:00 P.M. came I rushed to the gym, and the fact that there were almost two hundred boys sitting in the bleachers didn't even faze me. This was what I had been waiting for all those years in the Camanche grammar school —and I fully expected to make the team.

The coach arrived and went into his speech: "Now, boys, we're not going to look at size. We don't care how big you are—we're going to pick boys that look like winners—boys that can *win* for Linwood Junior High. Now boys, we're here to make men out of you, and we want you to know that everybody has a chance."

That was such an obvious setup for the disappointment that was to follow that even a seventh grader should have recognized it. But I believed it like it was the gospel. *Yeah,* I echoed his words in my mind, *you don't have to be big— you just have to be a winner!* I expected a drill, a tryout— a chance to prove I was a winner and make the team.

And would you believe what happened next? That coach stood right up there after finishing his pep talk and picked the team right on the spot. And he picked every big dude in the place! *Not one* smaller boy was chosen. I sat there in the bleachers and nearly broke my arm raising it, stretching it, trying to get the coach to see me while he went through the crowd saying, "Okay, we'll take you . . . and you . . . and you . . ." until he had picked the team.

Only one seventh-grader was chosen, and he was a big, fat kid whom I particularly disliked because he was rich and was always flashing his money around. I never had any money and I didn't like him; so, when he was picked for the team and I *wasn't,* it just topped off the whole tragic mess.

I went home and cried like a baby. My dad comforted me a little: "Don't worry, son, you'll get your chance someday. Just keep working hard and you'll get your chance." It helped my feelings when I discovered that I still had a year of eligibility left in a city league football program. I enrolled there and got to play quarterback on a team in that league, but even then I knew the difference between big time and small taters, and the city league was definitely small taters. As far as I was concerned, the year was a total wipe-out.

The next summer my family moved to a new school district, and I was delighted. I would be going to Oak Terrace Junior High, and this year everything would be different. When school started I was charged up and ready to go. Sure enough, toward the end of the first week at Oak Terrace, they started playing the same song, second verse. The announcement. The meeting in the gym. The monstrous crowd. The coach and his phoney-baloney pep talk: "Now, boys, don't think just because you're bigger than little Johnny you're going to be picked and Johnny isn't. We aren't paying any attention to size; we're going to pick boys who are willing to work hard and dedicate themselves. Don't think just the big boys are going to get those uniforms—we're going to give them to boys that will make the Trojans a winner!" And then came the process of picking the team ("you . . . you . . . you . . ."), and once again the coach selected the thirty biggest boys there.

I'll never forget how badly we wanted to get those uniforms. One fellow had wrecked his bicycle that day and poked the handlebar through his stomach, but he came to the meeting anyway, hoping to get a uniform. I sat in the bleachers and watched him holding a bandage over a big hole in his stomach, with the blood oozing around his fingers, and I couldn't take my eyes off him. And he, like me, raised his hand and yelled "Pick me!" in vain. When it was all over, "big" was beautiful, and I was nowhere.

Nothing to do but cry again, so I did again, and Dad consoled me again. The hurt was worse this time because lots of my eighth-grade friends had gotten uniforms, and I was now too old to play city league ball. I was only one year away from high school, and couldn't even make it as a scrub on the eighth-grade team!

There was one glimmer of hope—an outside chance, to be sure, but by now I was grasping at straws. The coach had said that those of us who hadn't made the team could come to the practices if we wanted to watch. I think the idea was that, if some of the big boys got hurt or mangled or killed or something, we would be there to step in. The first day of practice I didn't go because I was still so disappointed over being left off the team; but on the second day of practice, I went out after school to watch them work out.

I stood on the sidelines that afternoon and, boy, did I feel bad! All my buddies were out there practicing and I stood on the sidelines with a little wormy-looking kid thinking, "I'm five thousand times better than this guy and here we are both at exactly the same level." I was eating my heart out.

Somehow one of the footballs that the team was using bounced off the field right where we were standing. I may not have looked like a ballplayer but I was resourceful that day —I stepped in front of the ball so the guys on the field wouldn't see it, and eventually they quit looking and continued their drill without it.

I said, "C'mon, let's throw," to the boy beside me, and we began to throw the ball back and forth on the sidelines. I was enjoying it so much that I forgot about the practice and was just winging that ball. I cut a good one loose and looked up to see the coach standing out on the field, whistle in his mouth, watching me.

My big chance! My heart started beating double-time, and I knew I had to impress that coach. For the next ten minutes I did everything I knew how to do with a football and some things I had never thought of before. I threw it short. I threw it long. I threw it on the run, leaping into the air like a shortstop. I threw it so hard I also knocked holes in that little boy's chest. I ran to my right and threw, ran to my left and threw; every time heaving the ball as far as I could.

After about ten minutes, here came the coach, right off the playing field, right over to where I was. He grabbed me, put his arm around me, and said, "How did I miss you, son?" I acted surprised that he was watching and tried to be as nonchalant as possible; but when he told me to come by his office after practice to get a uniform, I just about went crazy!

I picked up my uniform and ran all the way home. I tore into the house screaming and hollering, jumping up and down, "I made it! I made it! I've got a uniform and I'm on the football team!" I hugged everybody, ran around the house like a crazy man—I just couldn't believe it. My dad had told me that if I ever made the team he would buy me a pair of football shoes, not those old nubby rubber things like I had been wearing, but real, sure-enough football shoes with cleats and a little white stripe down the side. He took me to get those Sears and Roebuck football shoes, and I could barely sleep that night.

The next day I put on my uniform and those shoes (nobody else had a pair like them) and trotted out toward the practice field, across an old concrete basketball court, my cleats clicking on the concrete, and I felt I had finally made it to the big time. My pants were about three sizes too big and twisted around my skinny little legs, but I didn't even notice. I thought everything was just *super,* and I was on top of the world!

Would you believe that coach put me on defense! That's right—middle linebacker! I couldn't understand it. I finally figured that he liked my arm and wanted me around in case his regular quarterback got hurt. I had never even *thought* about playing defense; but football was football, so I went at it with a vengeance.

For one day I was the meanest middle linebacker this side of Dick Butkus. I must have made seventeen unassisted tackles that day. I would tear through the offensive line, beat the center on the snap, and clobber the quarterback before he could get rid of the ball. I chased down ball carriers behind the line of scrimmage. I was a madman, going on pure adrenalin on every play.

I busted up my hands that afternoon—sprained about nine fingers—and they puffed up, big and painful. I got kicked under the eye, just enough to open a little cut, and that topped it all off and made everything perfect. I thought that cut was great. My mom asked me about it when I got home for supper. "A cut? Where? . . . oh, *that!* I must have got that in the game this afternoon, Mom." That made the day complete.

I played linebacker the rest of the year, getting in to play quarterback on a few occasions. The season wasn't a particularly memorable one, but I learned two things that year: one, that I could throw the ball. I had a strong arm and threw it hard and straight, and that year I learned to really cut the ball loose when I needed to. The second thing I learned was that defense was not for me. It beat sitting on the bench—but just barely. By the time the year was over, I was determined to be a quarterback. I wanted that glory position, that glamour position. I wanted to be in charge out on the field —to do something important on every play. By this time I was becoming a dyed-in-the-wool quarterback fan. Bart Starr of the Green Bay Packers and Johnny Unitas of the Baltimore Colts were my heroes. I watched them on television, tried to learn their moves, and dreamed of being a quarterback. Quarterback was the dream position and I wanted to play it.

Something else happened that season that affected my future. I broke my collarbone twice. Linebacker is a rough position, and I had more zeal than my physical equipment could stand. Twice I broke my left collarbone, so I really hit the weights. I started a weightlifting program, bought a set of barbells that I could use at home, and started working hard to build more muscle onto what was becoming a tall, lanky frame.

When I started the ninth grade—my last in junior high— I won the job as starting quarterback, but in the very first game of the season I dislocated my right shoulder. I handed off on a power sweep to the right and was running along, following the ball carrier, when I got wiped out from the blind side. I never even saw the guy. When that happened it scared me. I was afraid I was going to be injury-prone—that I was never going to stay healthy long enough to play good football. So I went back to the weights, determined to get back before the season was over.

We played only a seven-game schedule in junior high, but I made it back from that injury in five weeks, in time to start the last two games as quarterback.

When my sophomore year came, I entered Woodlawn High School in Shreveport, a large school (about twenty-three hundred students) that played on the AAA level of prep competition in the state of Louisiana. The coach there was Lee Hedges, and all he was interested in on the first day we sophomores showed up for practice was Mike Bates, a quarterback from another junior high school. He was a crackerjack passer and runner, and his reputation had preceded him to Woodlawn. I beat him out, beat him good, and when the season started I was the established sophomore quarterback.

Woodlawn had a *B* team for sophomores and juniors who couldn't make the varsity, and there it was that I saw all my action for the next two years. I was allowed to dress out for the varsity games, but the quarterback who started was too good for me to challenge him for the job. His name was Tray Prather, and he was an All-State and All-American high-school quarterback for those two years. The team was playing great, going to the playoffs every year, but I wasn't getting in on any of the action. I collected splinters on the bench and occasionally would get into the game for the last minute or two if we were ahead. Once, against Minden High School, we were ahead 33–7 and even then I didn't get into the game. Prather had a chance to set some kind of record, and Coach Hedges didn't want to pull him. I was like a young horse just chomping at the bit, and I resented not getting any playing time. I figured if the coach can't take a chance on you when you're ahead 33–7, when are you ever going to learn to play?

I was playing on the *B* team, and had a pretty good year. My rival for the starting quarterback position was Tommy Spinks, who had been my best friend since the eighth grade. Tommy was like a brother to me then, and still is. He was a good passer and ball handler, and it was always nip and tuck as to who would play quarterback after Tray Prather graduated. Toward the end of our junior year the coaches were really looking us over in those times that we got to play, and we were both well aware that we were being sized up for the next fall. During the last game, I was playing with instructions not to pass. I saw a man open and couldn't resist throwing to him. The pass dropped incomplete, and Coach Hedges was really mad. He pulled me and sent Spinks in. A little later Spinks had a man wide open in the end zone and missed him, so Coach Hedges pulled him and in I went again. I was determined to show him I could score with that ball, so on the very first down I called a deep pass play and threw a 40-yarder for a touchdown.

Coach Hedges was so pleased with the score that he forgot

to get mad at me for throwing against orders. I look back on that and realize how easily things could have turned out differently. If I had not completed that pass—or if Spinks had completed his—it might have changed my whole future. I honestly don't believe I would have had a chance to start at quarterback the next fall. I was stupid and bullheaded, but luck was with me and I came out smelling like a rose.

The varsity went to the state playoffs that year, Tray Prather graduated and signed a scholarship with Louisiana State University, and immediately all the fans and sportswriters in Shreveport began ringing the death bell for Woodlawn High football. Only one of twenty-two starters was returning to the squad, and everybody seemed to give up on the team for the next year. A "rebuilding year," they were calling it. Not much chance of winning very many games, but maybe some of the young kids would get some experience. One sportswriter went on record predicting that we would win only 3 out of our 10 games.

That made Tommy Spinks and me mad. Here we had spent the last two years playing on the *B* team while Tray Prather and all the big stars were on winning teams, going to the semifinals of the state playoffs, and becoming the heroes of Shreveport. Now finally our chance had come and everybody was talking about how we had no chance for a decent season! The more they talked about how bad we were going to be, the more determined we were to do whatever it took to win.

There was just one problem: we were both quarterbacks,

competing for the starting job. But Tommy wanted us to win so badly that he did one of the most selfless things I've ever seen in sports—he went to Coach Hedges and asked to be switched to wide receiver. He had only average speed, but had good hands and great moves, and he knew he could catch the ball and run with it. The coach said we could go ahead and try it that way, Bradshaw-to-Spinks, me throwing and him catching, instead of us both battling for the same position. That *yes* from Coach Hedges was all we needed to get started. Spinks and I came up with a slogan: WORK TO WIN—And all that winter and spring we *worked.*

We ran pass routes over and over, repeating every pass play in the Woodlawn offense until we could practically predict the moves each other made. Every Friday I spent the night with him, or he with me, and we talked about football, then got up on Saturday morning to practice. Football. Football. Football. That's all we thought about through the spring and summer. We even double-dated together and talked about football on our dates!

With Prather gone and Spinks at wide receiver, I was unchallenged as starting quarterback and leader of the team. The pressure of that responsibility seemed to bring the best out of me. Coach Hedges was a great quarterback coach, and over the years has developed some of the finest quarterbacks in the state of Louisiana. He worked hard with me that year, Spinks developed into an outstanding receiver, the rest of the team played 'way above everyone's expectation, and we had a great season.

One thing bothered me—I played quarterback all year and did not call a *single play* for myself. Coach Hedges believed in the system in which the coach calls the plays from the sidelines. We had alternating guards on the offensive line (messenger guards, they are sometimes called), and on each down one of them came running into the huddle with a play from Coach Hedges. I didn't like it then and I don't like it now. In my opinion, a quarterback is not a complete quarterback unless he calls his own plays.

Naturally, a quarterback expects the coach to call the shots on certain occasions when the game or a touchdown is at stake. But not *every* play! One of the things I appreciate about Chuck Noll, my head coach at the Pittsburgh Steelers, is that he gives me a good game plan and then leaves it to me to execute it, to call the plays out on the field as the game progresses. There are lots of things about the tempo and the "feel" of a game which only a quarterback is in a position to understand. A coach on the sideline just cannot possibly be as sensitive to what is taking place on the field as the man who is actually out there. Why do some coaches (even in pro football) insist on calling the plays? I think in some cases a coach, especially a former quarterback like Norm Van Brocklin of the Atlanta Falcons, tries to relive his playing days by calling the plays from the sidelines. Whatever their reasons for doing it, I don't think coaches who call the plays are giving their quarterbacks an opportunity to become complete ballplayers, and I think any quarterback in the National Football League will agree with me.

We started winning that senior year and by midway through the season, we knew we had a shot at the playoffs. We dropped one game and tied another late in the year, and finished the year with eight victories, a loss, and a tie—and, most importantly, a berth in the state playoffs.

I had a good year, with over 1400 yards passing and a 47 percent completion average, but was disappointed when I didn't receive any individual honors as a quarterback. As a matter of fact, I didn't even make the All-City team in Shreveport, that honor going to some sophomore across town whose team failed to make the playoffs. Tommy Spinks? He had a fabulous year as a receiver, catching 55 passes for 12 touchdowns and a new school record. He made All-City, All-District, and All-State teams, and deserved every bit of it.

We opened in the playoffs against South Terrebonne High School whom we had not beaten in ten years. We beat them 14–10, and moved on to the semifinals, where we were expected to be crunched by Lafayette, a team led by Ross Brupbacher. He was later to be an All-American linebacker at Texas A & M, and plays now with the Chicago Bears. We beat Lafayette badly, 28–13, and I had one of the best games of my high-school career. I passed for 176 yards, including two touchdowns, and ran for two more touchdowns. There were lots of college scouts in the stands that night, and that one game is probably what won me a college scholarship. Until that night I had heard not a word from any college scout, and I was scared to death that I wasn't going to be

offered a football scholarship. I was never flooded with doz-
ens of offers like so many players are, but the week after that
Lafayette game I heard from a couple of schools, so I knew
I was going to get something anyway.

The game for the AAA state football championship was
played between Woodlawn and Sulphur High School in a
driving rainstorm. Our defense trapped the Sulphur quarterback in the end zone for a safety early in the game, and we
scored a touchdown in a downpour to put us ahead 9–0. But
in the second half we just couldn't get anything done. Our
offense sputtered and slipped in the mud and never got going,
and we allowed two Sulphur touchdowns. When it was all
over, we had lost 12–9.

3
LSU or Tech?

AS THE GAME ENDED, I walked off the field in the rain, and Billy Laird, a former quarterback from Louisiana Tech, came up and put his arm around me, and told me he wanted me to sign a scholarship with Tech. I was all choked up over losing the game and didn't want to talk to him, so a Tech coach came over to the house the next day and gave me a big sales pitch for Louisiana Tech, a relatively small college in Ruston, Louisiana, which is about seventy-five miles from Shreveport. The next day I got a call from a local alumnus of Baylor University (Waco, Texas) wanting to talk to me about going there, and a couple of days later heard from Louisiana State University. A lot is written about blue-chip high-school athletes and the pressure exerted on them as different schools try to recruit them. I certainly was not a blue-chipper, and it probably was a good thing, because as it turned out I was so immature and eager to please that I barely handled the pressure of my piddling three offers.

First came a look at Baylor. I was a gung-ho Baptist, and a Christian, and I was interested in going to a Baptist school. On the other hand, I didn't particularly want to play in

Texas, so when I left Shreveport to fly out to Waco it was with mixed feelings. The weekend on campus ended the indecision in a hurry. I had a perfectly miserable weekend. I was awkward, straight-laced, and totally uncomfortable. They offered to get me a date with a Baylor girl, but I told them I had a girl friend back home. They took me to a party, but I was shy and out of sorts and asked to go back to my room. The next day was cold and dreary and I just sat in my room in this crummy-looking dormitory all day, miserable, homesick, staring at the walls. By the time I went home, I knew I never wanted to see Baylor again. Going out to Waco was my very first airplane ride, so I guess it wasn't a total loss.

Next I went to LSU, located down in Baton Rouge, Louisiana. There I got such a super sales job that by the end of my visit I would have signed anything. It was high-pressure all the way. They showed me all over the fabulous campus, talked to me about the great LSU football tradition, took me out to dinner with all the coaches. And their arguments were tailor-made for me.

Mostly they talked about the importance of going to a "major league" school, where I would be playing "with the best, against the best," as they put it. They made me feel like it would be cowardly to go to Louisiana Tech, where I would be playing small-college competition. "The only way you'll find out if you've really got the goods," they said, "is to come to LSU and play with the big boys." They made going to Tech sound like playing Pee-Wee League.

I was ripe, and I swallowed every argument without blinking. By the time I was ready to leave I promised them that I would sign and, a day or two after I got home, did just that, with the photographers and writers from the Shreveport papers duly recording the event.

Then the *real* pressure started. I didn't realize (until I signed with LSU) just how strongly so many people around Woodlawn High felt about Tech. First to express her displeasure was my girl friend, who called me on the phone when she heard I had signed with LSU and broke up with me. How's that for hitting a guy where it hurts! She had a brother at Tech and she planned to go there and she just didn't see how I could do such a horrible thing as to even *think* about going anywhere else. So she didn't want to date me anymore. So much for teeny-bopper logic! And so much for that particular romance!

Next came my backfield coach. When I got back from Baton Rouge he wouldn't talk to me for days. As more and more people began to fuss with me about going to LSU, I began to weaken. I got confused. When I had been at Baton Rouge, all the arguments for going there made sense to me, but now that I was back home it seemed more logical to go to Tech. I didn't know what to think anymore. My backfield coach started then, singing the praises of Tech for hours on end. He would invite me to go fishing with him, promising not to talk about college, and pump me full of Tech propaganda all day long. He told me that LSU was just a football factory, that the people there wouldn't take a personal interest in me, that they wouldn't help me graduate after my playing days were over. He told me that Tech was a passing team that would really use a passing quarterback, while LSU stayed with a running attack. He told me I needed to stay closer to Shreveport so my family could see me play more. And the more I listened, the more I was convinced I had made the wrong choice.

So I changed my mind. I called the Tech coaches, told them I wanted to sign with them, and they found a technicality which allowed me to do so. What had actually happened was that the LSU sales pitch about being a "big-league quarterback" had backfired. I was very insecure, was having terrible trouble with my self-confidence, and just wasn't ready for the high-pressure situation at a major university like LSU. To tell the truth, I was afraid I couldn't make it at LSU. I wanted to go where I could play, and I remembered that Tray Prather was there. I had sat on the bench most of my life, and when it got right down to it, I wanted to go to a school where my chances of being a starting quarterback were better than at LSU.

Looking back, it was the right decision—it was just reached in a clumsy, immature fashion. Down deep, I wanted to go to Tech all along, but I was so flattered by LSU's attention and so impressed by things at Baton Rouge that I almost made the mistake of my life, just because I was too overwhelmed to say *no.* Tech was the right school for me; it gave me time to get some of the experience I had missed by not starting in high school without the pressure of major college ball. It also had a wide-open passing offense which allowed me to do plenty of what I did best—throw the ball.

The toughest thing I ever did in my life was to tell LSU head coach Charley McLendon—absolutely a great man— that I was not coming to LSU. I played in a high school All-Star game on the LSU campus a few weeks later, and went by Coach McLendon's office and laid the word on him. Then I went out, played the football game, and passed out from heat prostration and had to be hospitalized. I'll never know how much of it was due to heat prostration, and how much was due to that meeting with Coach McLendon!

4
Javelin Champ

AN IRONIC THING about my high-school days is that my football career was completely overshadowed by my participation on the Woodlawn track team as a javelin thrower. Coach A. L. Williams, the track-and-field coach, saw that I had a strong arm and asked me to throw the javelin. My buddy Spinks was a pole-vaulter on the team, so I decided to give it a try. At first I didn't like it at all. Coach Williams gave me a javelin and led me out to an area away from the rest of the team and pretty much said, "Here, throw it." No instruction, no coaching, no nothing. I got lonesome and bored stuck way off out there by myself, and I didn't like it. I would sneak off and go over to where the pole-vaulters were just about every day. And, just about every day, I would get caught and have to run laps. I don't know why I didn't quit long before the first track meet.

Ah, that first track meet! Up until the day of the City Meet I had received virtually no coaching, and I had no idea what I was doing. All I knew was that it was a long pole with a sharp point and the idea was to see how far you could throw it. Coach Williams came up to me the day of the meet and said, "Your arm feel all right?"

"Yeah."

"You been working out?"

"Yeah."

"You got your steps down?"

"Yeah."

"All right, let's go."

And off we went to the City Meet and one of the all-time low points in the history of track and field. I embarrassed Coach Williams, myself, Woodlawn High School, and all the descendants of whoever invented the javelin. There was a big crowd watching when it came my turn to throw. I ran down toward the line as fast as I could go, just flying on those skinny legs, full speed, until I got to the line. Then I slammed on the brakes, came to a screeching halt, and turned that thing loose standing stock-still at the line. No form, no technique, and I almost fell down when I threw it. The crowd laughed and my face turned beet-red under my flattop. The next four throws were just the same—full speed until I'd get to the line, lurched to a sudden stop, and then threw. When the dust had settled and the giggles had died, I had thrown the javelin 142 feet. That was good enough for dead last, 20 feet behind my closest competitor.

Coach Williams was really hot, and told me on the way home to get ready to work. But when he finished chewing me out, he was still embarrassed enough that my days of being ignored at practice were over. He began to coach me every afternoon, and I began to enjoy practice more than I had before. I eventually got up to 155 feet, 160 feet, and then suddenly to 170 feet—I was starting to get third place in some track meets, winning points for the Woodlawn team.

By the time the District Meet came around I was really getting the taste of throwing the javelin, and I was getting hungrier to throw really well. The meet was a preliminary one for the state finals in Baton Rouge, with the top two finishers in each event qualifying to go. I wanted to go so badly I could taste it. I was next to last in order of competition, and by the time my turn came, I had to have a throw of 168 feet to place second. I got a good one off—175 feet and 1 inch, but now the last entrant came up to throw and I thought I was done for. He was a fine javelin man, and had been winning meets all year with throws of up to 190 feet! It looked like a sure thing for him—and all I could do was sit on the sideline and cross my fingers.

When his last throw hit the ground it was an even 175 feet, and I had finished second and qualified for the State Meet. I'll never forget one thing about that day. The boy's daddy was one of those loud, swaggering guys who followed his son around to all the track meets and got on everybody's nerves. Always "My boy . . ." this and "My boy . . ." that—just a really obnoxious character. When his son finished third he exploded. "You let me down, you sorry so and so . . . ," he went on and on, berating the poor boy, cussing him out in front of all those people.

I was almost too excited to notice. I jumped up and down, screamed and hollered, hugged Tommy Spinks (who had qualified for the State Meet in the broad jump), and just generally went crazy. I couldn't believe it! Me going to the State Meet in the javelin throw! At the time I was so happy I almost thought that it was as important as football.

The State Meet was at LSU and we did the typical stupid, adolescent thing. We stayed up all night, horsing around in our hotel room, and when the meet started we were all about to fall down we were so exhausted. I didn't even qualify for the finals, and was almost too tired to care.

That was my sophomore year. When track season rolled around the next year, I was serious about becoming a good javelin thrower, and I worked hard. I threw distances of about 180 feet all year long and won most of my meets. Finally came the end of the season and time for the District Meet, and who, do you suppose, showed up but the same guy I had beaten out the year before! He had been winning his meets too, but with throws of 200, 202, 206 feet; so I figured I was going to take second. When the javelin throw started, I looked over at the crowd and there was that old man again, my rival's daddy, just as loud and nasty as ever. "My boy's gonna win this thing . . . my boy's great . . . my boy's been throwing 210 feet. . . ." I could hear him popping off all through the competition.

Finally it came down to me and that boy again. His first throw was an even 200 feet—a beautiful throw that nearly took my breath. I had never seen a javelin thrown that far in my life. My time came and I had nothing to lose, so I just closed my eyes and let the javelin go with all I had. It seemed like it stayed in the air five minutes, and when it hit it was sticking in the ground 200 feet, 2 inches away. I had won first place in the district! You could hear that old man all over the stadium, cussing me, his son, the officials, the crowd, the stadium, anybody he could think of. I was afraid for a minute he was going to come out there and slug me or something. He embarrassed his son so badly I'm surprised the kid kept competing.

I look back at that picture of that grouchy, profane, over-protective father in the stadium that day, and it makes me thankful for my parents and their attitude toward my athletic career. They are both proud of me—no doubt about it—and they would do anything to help me. But they have never followed me around, fawned over me, babied me, and tried to get kicks from my accomplishments. My mother is very excitable—that is probably where my emotional streak comes from—she roots for me and then lets the chips fall where they may. If I win that's great; and if I lose, that's all right too. My dad is the same way. He gives me plenty of support, but no pressure.

I hear criticism occasionally against Little League sports programs because they supposedly put so much pressure on the kids. I think that criticism is undeserved. If anything is at fault, it is the parents, not the program. Parents who smother their children with all kinds of athletic goals and expectations should not be surprised when their kids choke in the big games and end up hating sports in general. I think that parents should let the kids play, let the coaches coach, and be there to lend their support however things turn out.

My parents were that way, and I am grateful to them for it.

When my senior season came, I was ready. I had gotten bigger and stronger and more confident, and I felt like I was going to beat everybody I threw against. In the first meet of the year, the City Meet, I threw 217 feet. Unbelievable! I just *couldn't* believe it! I was "outstanding field man" for the meet, and was off to a good start. In the next meet, at the Fair Park Relays, I threw the javelin 243 feet, 7 inches for a new national high-school record. (I learned later that the previous record had been 232 feet, held by somebody in Washington.) *Well, maybe that was a fluke,* I thought, but the next week I threw 244 feet again. The next week came the Bossier Relays, and I made seven throws of over 239 feet, each of which beat the national record that had stood two weeks earlier. I still don't know exactly what happened, but somehow things just came together, and throwing 230 feet seemed easy. I broke my own national record several times and got my picture in *Sports Illustrated.*

Then I hurt my elbow, and it was all over. It was in the Airline Relays, and I slipped as I threw; I got it away pretty well, but had to do it all with my arm and tore something up inside my elbow. I only got one good one away after that —256 feet in the Woodlawn Relays—and it landed flat. My arm was killing me every time I threw the thing. My distances dropped down to the 210–215 range, and I was just hanging on until the end of the season. I was still winning, but it was painful to throw, and after you've been up to 240, 210 is no fun even if it wins the meet.

Finally the State Meet arrived, and I wanted to get one more good throw out of that arm to break the record for the State Meet. I rested the elbow as much as I could before the meet, and applied hot-and-cold, ice-and-whirlpool treatments for two weeks prior to the meet. I knew all I needed was one good throw to set the new record. I got myself all psyched up, went tearing down the runway on my first try, and threw it 239 feet 11 inches—a new record. I put my pole in my bag, zipped it up, and went up and sat in the stands for the rest of the event. One throw and that was it. I've never thrown the javelin since that day. I had done what I could, the challenge was gone, my elbow was aching, and throwing the javelin had lost all its appeal.

I'm lucky that I didn't mess up my elbow so badly that it hurt me in football. Most of the credit goes to a really terrific trainer, my brother Gary. He was the team trainer at Woodlawn, got a full scholarship as a trainer to Louisiana Tech, and took good care of me all the way through. It was like having my own personal doctor. He took as much pride in what I accomplished as if he had done it himself, and he probably saved me from wrecking my arm.

I got over two hundred scholarship offers to throw the javelin at colleges all over the country. I didn't even consider them. As far as I was concerned, the javelin was trifling and unimportant compared to football. I was bound for Louisiana Tech to play football. I had been pointing toward pro football since the second grade, and the next step along the way was college ball. I wanted to succeed as a college quarterback more than anything in the world, and now it was time to see if I had what it took. Nothing else mattered.

5
Lowly Frosh at Tech

IF YOU EVER HAVE occasion to visit Ruston, Louisiana, prepare to find a typical small, Southern town set in the most beautiful countryside in the state. Louisiana Tech is a bustling, growing campus of about seventy-five hundred students, a part of the state university system.

I arrived on campus in late August. As a member of the college division of the National Collegiate Athletic Association, Tech was allowed to play freshmen on its varsity team, and consequently did not field a separate freshman team. That was good and bad: good because I started right off with the varsity; bad because I started in a position with which I was already abundantly familiar—the bench.

Tommy Spinks had also signed a scholarship with Tech, and he and I went there together in high hopes of making a dent in the squad in our freshman year. In the very first play of the very first scrimmage I threw my very first pass to Tommy, a short angle-in route. I was so eager to impress the coaches that I threw it as hard as I could, and Tommy made a diving catch and hung onto the ball. He made me look sharp, and it was a good omen.

Unfortunately, that was just about the highlight of the year for me. Spinks got quite a bit of playing time as a freshman, and by his sophomore year had a starting position nailed down. With me it was a little harder. Tech's head coach already had settled on his starting quarterback for the year, a sophomore named Phil Robertson. There were a couple of other quarterbacks on the team, but I worked hard and quickly moved ahead of them to claim the number two spot. And work is what it took, too, since the Tech offense was built around a pro-football model, and was extremely complicated. I found the transition from good ol' simple Woodlawn to Tech a tough one mentally. I had to study, study, study to learn all the different plays, sets, formations, and keys. The best thing about that freshman year was that nothing was expected of me, so there was no pressure. Every week the same pattern: I studied hard, prepared myself, then stood on the sidelines on Saturday while Robertson ran the team.

Louisiana Tech was at the time a member of the Gulf States Conference, a league of ten college-division teams in Louisiana. There were no Notre Dames or Alabamas in the conference, but there were good, tough teams; and the Louisiana Tech Bulldogs, 1965 edition, went out on the field every Saturday and got our faces kicked in. Our record for the year was one win and nine losses. We always lost the close ones. (And we always lost those that weren't so close, too.)

As the year wore on, I became totally dissatisfied with the situation. It was not just that we were losing, or just that I wasn't getting to play. It was that I was not getting a chance to show what I could or couldn't do. Every game Phil Robertson started; every game we lost; and still the coach stuck with him! I felt like I was a better quarterback than he was, and if I had a fair shot at the job I would have beaten him out, but that opportunity never came. Only once did I get to play the major part of a game. That was the Homecoming Game against Southeastern Louisiana, when Robertson was hurt and I came in to play good, solid ball and lead the team to our only victory of the season. I expected to start the next game after that, but when Saturday rolled around I was right back on that familiar old spot—the bench—just as if the game a week before had never happened.

When that freshman season ended I was disappointed with Tech and felt that I was destined to spend my college career on the bench. During the off-season, Coach Joe Aillet, who had directed the football team at Tech for many years, announced his resignation as coach and Maxie Lambright was appointed to replace him. Lambright was an unknown quantity at Tech, but his reputation was that of a three-yards-in-a-cloud-of-dust man, a coach who favored a conservative, running offense over the passing game. So I began to look elsewhere.

I was very much impressed with Florida State University and their wide-open approach to offense. They didn't just talk about throwing the ball—they *threw* it, and their offense was as near to a pro offense as that of any college team in the country. I decided to try to transfer to Florida State for the rest of my college career. It would mean sitting out my sophomore year, but the way things were going for me at Tech that would hardly have been a sacrifice.

I got in touch with the coaches at Florida State and told them what I had in mind. They seemed to like the idea and were very encouraging, urging me to come to the campus and work out the details as soon as possible. That was all the encouragement I needed. I got in my car and drove all the way to Tallahassee. When I got there, it was (as they say) a whole new ball game. The coaches who had seemed so cordial and encouraging earlier didn't act the least bit interested in my plans to transfer, and the head coach Bill Peterson (now with the Houston Oilers) hastened to tell me in no uncertain terms to get myself back up to Louisiana Tech and not to bother coming back.

I never will know for sure what happened between the time I left Ruston and the time I arrived in Tallahassee to produce such a dramatic change in the attitude of the FSU coaches. Maybe they just changed their minds, but I doubt it. I have always suspected that somehow the coach at Tech got wind of what I was doing (I had told some of my teammates), and called Peterson or one of the other coaches at Florida State, putting pressure on them not to cooperate with my plan to change schools. I don't know it for sure, but it is my guess that that's what happened. So I returned to Tech, prepared to spend the next two years watching Robertson hand the ball to the running backs. I had a surprise waiting for me. In his first meeting with the squad, Lambright prom-

ised that he was going to put every job on the team up for
grabs, and that whoever proved he could win the job would
get to start. He was as good as his word. When football drills
started the next fall there was no depth chart, no first-string-
ers or second-stringers—just football players, and whoever
proved he could play would play.

And so it turned out that, while I was running around
trying to leave the problem, the problem left me. I had been
rebuffed at Florida State and came home to find that the
situation I was attempting to escape had been unexpectedly
changed in just the direction that I wanted. The way everything turned out, I was lucky on both ends of the deal!

6
The Blond Bommuh

AND SO MY SOPHOMORE year was one of gradual improvement, both of my skills as a quarterback and of my position on the team. I didn't beat Robertson out of the starting job immediately, but from the very start of the season I got lots of playing time, and made a strong challenge for the starting position. By the end of the year, I had passed for 951 yards and was confident that I would be starting the next fall.

Robertson was quite a character—one of those players who was blessed with great ability—but somehow never seemed to take the game seriously enough to be a winner. All through the two years that we played together, he seemed to be interested in everything *but* football. He was a real hunting and fishing nut, and that's all he talked about—in practice, in the locker room, always talking about the fish he caught or the ducks he shot. The football game always seemed secondary. He would stroll into the locker room an hour before game time with blood on his clothes and squirrel guts hanging out of his pockets and say, "Let's see, who are we playing today?" Then he would laugh and talk about his hunting trip that morning while he dressed for the game.

It wasn't just Robertson who had this attitude; it was lots of the older members of the team. We would go out on the field and get bombed about 38–0 and come back into the locker room at half time and these guys would sit around and talk about duck hunting until time to go back out and get plastered for two more quarters. It was unbelievable. We were losers and some of the guys didn't even seem to care. We went 3–7 that year and I lay the blame purely on that losing attitude. We had a bunch of seniors who didn't care anything about winning—and that is why we didn't win.

Robertson never seemed to resent the fact that I was crowding him for the starting job in that sophomore year, and often teased me about my enthusiasm and my success in throwing the long bomb. One day, after I had thrown a long touchdown pass, he came into the locker room and said, "Man, you really bombed them today, Bradshaw." He laughed as I took off my helmet and continued, "You are really the big bommuh on this team, Bradshaw. *Bommuh,* that's what we ought to call you. Bradshaw, the Blond Bommuh!" He liked the title and started calling me the Blond Bomber from that day on, and that is where the newspapers picked up the nickname that they used so frequently the next two years.

Phil Robertson quit the team after that year. I never really understood the guy, but when he left, the starting quarterback job was mine for keeps; and *that* I understood. I began to feel the pressure to produce a winner for the first time since I had arrived in college.

When fall practice began my junior year, it seemed that things were different from the very first workout. We had lots of young, aggressive players on the team who had not inherited that losing attitude from the players who had graduated. We felt that we could really be good—could play winning football all year long. We had been picked in the preseason polls to finish last in the Gulf States Conference; and, based on the 4–16 record for the past two years, that was not an unreasonable prediction. But I don't believe there was a man on the team who thought there was even a chance that we would be that bad.

We had some real gutsy ballplayers at Tech that year. Spinks was going into his second year as a starting receiver. He wasn't fast, but he had developed into one of the shiftiest ends in the conference, with hands like gluepaper and a great ability to catch the ball off balance and hang on. Another great receiver was Larry Brewer, who was also my roommate. Brewer loved to catch the ball so much that the guys on the team accused him of being extra nice to me so that I would throw to him more often. They called him my shadow, and kidded him unmercifully about his inability to run the "Bulldog Mile" in conditioning drills and his inability to tolerate pain. He was a big cutup, and always called the coaches by their first names. A third fine receiver was Ken Liberto, another product of Woodlawn High in Shreveport. We had two good running backs in Bubba Sanchez (short but a gutty runner with powerful legs) and Buster Herren, an extremely quick scatback who ran like his shirttail was on fire and was one of the hardest fellows I've ever seen to bring down in the open field.

The season started and we were as good as we thought we could be. We opened on the road against Mississippi State, a major college team and a member of the almighty Southeastern Conference. We played them tough and with 2:21 left on the clock in the last quarter the score was knotted at 13–13. We pushed into Mississippi State territory, down as far as their 37-yard line with a first down. I threw incomplete once. I threw incomplete twice. I threw incomplete three times. And then on 4th-and-10 I hit Spinks with the ball down the sideline and he sailed all the way into the end zone for a touchdown that gave us a big 20–13 upset victory. It was a sweet one to chalk up for my first college start.

Nervousness is as unpredictable as a kid crossing the street. I suppose if someone ever comes up with a sure-fire explanation for why people get nervous, he'll make a million dollars. I should have been nervous in that Mississippi State game—season opener, my first start, major college opponent —but I was relaxed, calm, loose as a goose. Then the next week we played East Carolina and, with a win under my belt, I should have been relaxed, but it didn't work out that way. We played at home, the opening game of a new stadium at Tech, and I was nervous as a crook at a hanging, and didn't sleep well the night before. I started the game tight and uncomfortable, and though I didn't throw well, we won in a romp. I left the game in the 3rd quarter with a 26–0 lead, and we finally beat them 35–7.

We lost the next two games, both of them to conference rivals. We played McNeese State in our conference opener, and in the first half I practically stunk up the stadium, I was so bad. It was the first time in my life I had started a game and played so poorly. I was overthrowing receivers who were wide open, throwing behind receivers into the arms of the defensive backs, bobbling the ball on handoffs to the running backs. You name it—and if it was wrong—I did it that day in the first half. We went into the locker room at half time behind 20–0; I had thrown 16 passes, completed four and had four intercepted.

When I went in at half time I was so upset with myself I was almost physically sick. I got off in the corner of the locker room, away from the rest of the team, and talked to myself: "Listen, you big dummy, what's wrong with you? Here you are running around thinking about being a pro quarterback and you can't even complete a pass against McNeese State. Now you go out there in the second half and you throw that stupid ball like you know how to throw it. Just hang loose and lay it in there to Spinks like you did in high school. It's no different now, so get out there and do it!" I chastised and exhorted myself like that until time to go back out, and when I hit the field for the second half, I was ready.

I called a pass play to Spinks, hit him right on the numbers with the ball, and we were rolling. I threw fourteen consecutive completions after that; I was drilling the ball and the receivers were making tough catches look easy. When it was all over we had lost the game 27–20, but in the showers afterwards none of us felt too badly about it. We had proved to ourselves that we could get up off the floor and come back on a tough team, that we were not quitters—and our morale was surprisingly high after the loss.

I learned something that day, and everything I have seen and experienced since has only confirmed it: Football is an emotional game—a mental, psychic game—a game you play more with your adrenalin than with your muscles. I am convinced that the best coached, most perfectly built physical specimen in the world can be totally useless on a football field if he has all kinds of negative vibrations at work in his mind and his emotions. On the other hand, you could let the scrawniest little kid in town put a football under his arm and, if his vibrations are right and his juices are really flowing, he'll run over guys twice his size.

Football is played primarily between your ears. Especially for a quarterback, who handles the ball on every play and throws it a lot, the emotional part of the game is about half of it. In the pros, every quarterback in the league has the physical qualities and the technical skills to be a winner, so the championships go to the quarterback who can generate the most emotional intensity on the field and still keep that calm, cool control over the game. In that McNeese State game, I learned that I could do anything if I got my head straight. That second half got me over the hump, and I was on my way to a dream season as a quarterback.

The next week the Ragin' Cajuns of Southwestern Louisiana came in, and we had an old-fashioned, head-bustin' football game. Our offense was really rolling, but so was theirs, and we traded the lead back and forth all day.

It was one of those hot, sticky Louisiana days, and by the beginning of the fourth quarter both teams were beginning to slow down. I got hit hard on a quarterback keeper and had to be led off the field—the blow and the exhaustion from the heat combining to make me too weak to play. Then a flukey thing happened that cost us the 24–21 lead that we held at the time. Our defense had held them with only three or four minutes to play, and had forced them to punt. The Southwestern kicker laid it up real high and, when it hit, it took a crazy bounce on the turf, caromed off the *back* of Ronnie Wiggins, one of our players, and was covered by Southwestern inside our 10-yard line! Four plays later they pushed the ball into the end zone to go ahead 28–24 with less than two minutes on the clock.

I was still pretty woozy, but now the game was in sudden danger of being lost, and in I went again. We put together one of those classic, last-minute drives. We ran the kickoff out to our own 33-yard line and took over there. On the next five plays, I hit Tommy Spinks on five consecutive complete passes. He was like a demon when he caught the ball and in those five plays—*bang! bang! bang!*—we went 60 yards from our own 33 to the Southwestern 7-yard line, first-and-goal with about thirty seconds to play.

And then the magic stopped. Incomplete pass. Running play to the right side for no gain. Two more incomplete passes into the end zone, and the game was over and we had lost 28–24. We came all that way, and then couldn't get the ball into the end zone. In the game I had gone 28 of 47 in passing for 432 yards to set two new conference passing records, but we had lost a game we played well enough to win, and we were all shellshocked. I told a reporter who asked me about the new conference records that day, "Records are for the birds if you can't win," and I think any quarterback worth his chinstrap would have agreed with me. Whoever said, "It matters not whether you win or lose, but how you play the game" had never lost 28–24 on a freaky bounce of the ball and a drive that stalled on the 7-yard line!

We were now 2–2 and things were beginning to smell a lot like last year. We didn't like it and we worked harder that week in practice than we had all season. The game coming up was the biggest of the year—any year. It was the annual game between Tech and Northwestern Louisiana, played at the State Fairgrounds Stadium in Shreveport. Northwestern was Tech's most bitter rival—the team we most loved to beat; and when the nighttime kickoff came there were thirty thousand people in the stands (which, for the Gulf States Conference, is a monstrously large crowd).

The night before the game I had a dream. I dreamed that we would win the game on a long touchdown pass that would bring us from behind with the final seconds running out on the clock. I would have paid no attention to that dream except that I had often dreamed things before that happened just as I had dreamed them.

I believed—and still do—that I have some kind of ESP

that sometimes lets me see future things in my dreams. So I didn't just dismiss that dream as a product of too much supper and pregame nerves. I took it seriously.

The game started out to be a rout for Northwestern. I had another one of those miserable first halves, throwing twelve times and completing only two of them. It seemed like our offense just couldn't get anything going, and at half time we were down 19–7.

The second half was a different story. Our attack began to jell on the first series, and I started clicking with my receivers, hit 11 of 17 passes in the 3rd quarter, and we got back into the ball game. It turned into a spectacular offensive show (896 total yards by both teams), and that big crowd reacted to every play as the battle shifted back and forth across the field.

With about three minutes remaining in the game, we were still trailing by a score of 39–35, when we put together a great clutch drive, moving the ball from our territory down to inside their 10-yard line. It looked like we were marching right into the end zone for the touchdown that would win the game. With 1:40 remaining, I rolled out to throw, was pressured by the defensive end, saw Larry Brewer in the end zone, and unloaded. Interception! I couldn't believe it—I mean, this couldn't happen to us two weeks in a row!

I came back to the bench with tears in my eyes; I was sick. I knew we probably would not get the ball back, and I couldn't believe that we had played so well and now were going to lose. Then I remembered that dream.

Well, the defense did its job. Northwestern took over on

its 20-yard line and our defense stopped them cold. Their kicker got a great punt away—it rolled and bounced and finally came dead on our 18-yard line with 13 seconds left on the clock. The offense trotted onto the field and Northwestern went into a "prevent" defense to guard against the only thing that could beat them—a long bomb. In the huddle I told my wide receivers to "just take off." It was going to take a miracle to win the game, so we might as well throw the playbook away and give it a chance to happen.

I took the ball from center and rolled out to my left, stopped, and saw Spinks about 20 yards upfield chugging along with two defenders right with him. As I set to throw, I saw Ken Liberto across the field going like a ball of fire with the Northwestern safety half a step behind. I turned it loose. It was right on target a mile down the field and the defender leaped up just as it got there. It went right through his hands, Ken caught it on his fingertips and stumbled into the end zone, and that crowd went so crazy I thought they were going to tear up half of Shreveport.

Oh, what a sweet victory! It was an 82-yard touchdown pass, the second longest in Tech history, and we won the game 42–39. I was so excited I hugged everybody in sight— Liberto, the defense, Spinks, the offensive line, anybody in a Tech jersey I could find and grab.

After that game we went undefeated for the rest of the season. The offense that we put together that night just kept getting better and better, and by the end of the year we were rolling over every team on our schedule. Something else happened after that game: I began to get in the national rankings for passing offense and total offense. The week after the Northwestern game was the first time I remember being in the race for offensive statistics as a quarterback; I was listed as 5th in the nation in total offense that week.

We went to Southern Mississippi for the next game and Liberto took up where he left off the week before. On the very first play of the game, he caught a little short pass, broke a couple of tackles, and went all the way for a 70-yard touchdown to put us ahead. We never fell behind. My next seven passes were complete (all for first downs or TDs), and I went 15–33 for 248 yards in the game to set all-time passing records for Tech and the conference for a single season. We beat them 27–20.

The next week we started a four-game closing streak in which we outscored our opponents 136–48. We beat Southeastern 35–7—Spinks catching 7 passes for 99 yards and Liberto 6 passes for 92 yards. Again the offense was hot—I went 26 of 48 for 389 yards, and it seemed like we always had the big play when we needed it.

7
The Good Ol' Days

OH, THOSE WERE THE GOOD OL' DAYS! We beat Lamar Tech
the next week 34–7, beat Northeastern 25–10, and were getting national attention for our powerful offense. The team
went to the top of the national offensive statistics, and I went
right along with them to the top of the individual passing
statistics. Reporters and pro scouts began popping up out of
the woodwork. At every game there were people from the
press and the NFL teams to watch us, and we never disappointed them. They started calling me the Bayou Bomber,
the Blond Bomber, the Rifleman, Bazooka Arm, and such
things. We were riding high and we loved it—after 1–9 and
3–7 seasons, you'd better believe we loved it!

We came into our last game of the season 7–2, with the
remaining contest set for Thanksgiving night, a tough one at
home against New Mexico State. This was a game that (when
the season began) everyone had already chalked up as a loss.
New Mexico State was big and tough, bigger than any team
we had played. They had these huge defensive linemen—like
6'7", 270 pounds—they were bigger than anyone we had
played against. A month or two earlier we wouldn't have

been given a chance, but now we were hot and we thought we could win it.

When the game started, we were tempted to change our minds. Their defensive line just beat us to death for the first quarter. They ran right over us. After falling behind early, our offensive line made some adjustments in its blocking, the pass protection stiffened, and we turned the game around on them. Without that big rush their pass defense wilted, and we had a field day the rest of the game. We beat them 42–24, with 445 yards passing. It was a perfect way to close out the season and, to add a little icing on the cake, we received an invitation to the Grantland Rice Bowl, the first bowl bid in Tech history.

To be honest about it, the Grantland Rice Bowl was something of an anticlimax after the great regular-season finish we had made. The game was played in Murfreesboro, Tennessee, that year, three weeks after the game with New Mexico, and it was nationally televised by one of the major networks, ABC. The game traditionally determines the unofficial national small college champion, and our opponent was Akron University. They had a reputation as a tough team, but by that time we felt like we could beat anybody.

When kickoff time came it was cold enough to freeze us Louisiana boys right into forty iceblocks. There was a 35 mile-an-hour wind blowing across that stadium floor and I had never been so cold in my life. We were accustomed to that good ol' down-South weather, even for football, and getting warmed up before the game was a real problem.

Being on national television was another novelty for us, and in the first quarter the whole team was tight and clumsy. After we got used to the cold and the idea of being on TV, we began to percolate just like we had all those Saturdays back home; and when we did it was Katy-bar-the-door for the Akron defense. We set four Grantland Rice Bowl records in a 33–13 romp. I had 19 completions in 33 attempts, and that rascal Spinks caught 12 of them. I was awarded the Most-Valuable-Player trophy for the game, and ended the season as the leading quarterback in the country in passing and total yardage, with the team leading the country in average yardage at 459 yards per game.

It had been one of those dream seasons, and the next year was to be just as good. That junior year was probably the key to my football career. It was my first year to start, the first year for Tech to gain national recognition, and the year that triggered the flood of newspaper stories and attention that would eventually land me in the pros. During those first two seasons I had begun to worry about the possibility of ever being drafted by the pros. When you're playing spasmodically for a small, unknown college that is going 1–9 and 3–7, the pro scouts just aren't going to come around. Several times before that junior year, I almost gave up on the hope of ever going to the pros, but by the time the junior season was over I never worried about it again. I knew that the pros would find me, that I would be drafted, and if I had a good senior year, I would be drafted high. So I just tried to forget about pro football and get ready to have a good last year at Tech.

It wasn't easy. When fall drills started, the pro scouts were crawling all over the place, and the newspapers and magazines were full of speculation on how high I would go in the pro draft that winter. Again I felt my mind wandering away from that dusty old practice field at Ruston, Louisiana, to the glamour and excitement of the National Football League. I had to fight with myself not to think about pro ball—to get my mind on the season coming up at Tech. I realized that it was important to my teammates to win the conference championship and have a big season. *Most of these guys won't be playing football anymore after this year,* I thought, *and it's not fair of me to be looking ahead of this season right here and now.*

In that regard, I have to give my coaches credit for doing a great job keeping me on an even keel. I think they realized how dangerous it would be for me to get to thinking ahead, so they just kept me from knowing about lots of the scouts who came around and things they said about me. They also tried to keep me from seeing many articles on me that were written in the papers and magazines. Many of the rave reviews that I got in college I never knew about until later. They did a good job protecting me from the natural tendency of feeling like Mr. Cool instead of working hard.

Occasionally one of those newspaper stories that I *did* see asked the question: "Was it all a fluke?" in discussing my junior year. As we got closer to the opening game, my passing still was not sharp and I began to worry. *After all,* I reasoned, *it was all pretty sudden. Maybe it* was *a fluke. Maybe I don't have it after all.* My self-confidence began to erode, and I began to press, and my passing got worse and worse. I just was not throwing the ball well, and I was afraid when the season started and the pressure was on that I was going to be exposed to the country as a flash-in-the-pan, one-shot quarterback.

We opened with a victory over East Carolina, and I came out looking okay without really throwing well at any time in the game. I passed for three touchdowns and that looked good on the stat sheets, but none of the TDs were really my doing. On the first one I hit Spinks on a short little sideline pattern, and he broke three tackles and turned what should have been a 7-yard gain into an 80-yard touchdown. Then I had Robby Albright wide open behind the secondary and underthrew him badly. He had to stop and wait on the ball, but made a little juke step, and turned on his 9.5 speed and outran everybody into the end zone. A little later I threw a wounded-duck lob into a crowd in the end zone, and one of my receivers jumped up and caught it for the score.

That day I could have kicked a dog and made ten dollars. Everything I did bad turned out good. I threw nothing but bad passes all day and wound up with 3 TDs and a ton of yardage. That's the way it is sometimes, and when things work out that way there is nothing to do but count your blessings and go about your business. On another day, you might hit your receivers in the chest with the ball and it pops loose and is intercepted. You might lay long bombs in their arms all day and have them dropped. It all evens out, they say, and I guess it does.

Anyway, the papers were saying what a fantastic start I was off to again, and I knew that I hadn't thrown a decent pass all year. We played McNeese State next and I threw the ball a little better, but still didn't feel good about it—likewise in the third game. I was completing passes and we were winning, but I just didn't have the feel—I didn't have a sense of controlling the ball when I turned it loose. Even when the ball went where I wanted it to go, it didn't have that good feel. It is a difficult thing to explain. Other people would see me throw and talk about how good it looked, but I knew it just wasn't right. It's something like a pro golfer such as Jack Nicklaus hitting a tee shot. The ball might fly out there 300 yards and everybody *oohs* and *ahs,* but Nicklaus doesn't feel good about it. You might insist that he hit it great, but he knows better. That's something like the way I felt in those first few games my senior year.

Then, suddenly—sometime during the fourth game—I was there. I struggled along and fought it and tried to work it out and then, *Bingo!* I was there. I started cutting the ball loose like I had the year before and we kept on winning. As a matter of fact, we beat everybody so badly that I hardly played in the 4th quarter of any game all year. I finished the season with total yardage of about 2,500 yards (as opposed to 2,900 yards the year before), and some people talked about my having a "disappointing season" because I didn't match my record as a junior. That was ridiculous, of course. I wasn't playing much more than half of each game, and if the games had been close I would have been in there all the way and gone over 3,000 yards easily. I remember one night at the University of Chattanooga, I came on hot as a two-dollar pistol and completed eleven passes in a little more than the 1st quarter. Then the coach pulled me out and I stood on the sidelines for the rest of the game.

I'll have to admit that I got frustrated that year. I didn't like spending so much time on the sidelines, no matter how far ahead we were. It had nothing to do with a desire to set any passing records, or lead the country in yardage, or anything like that. It was just that I wanted to play—plain and simple. Golly, I had spent most of my life sitting on the bench while somebody started ahead of me, and now here I was sitting out half the game every week so somebody *behind* me could get more experience! From the coach's standpoint it was the right thing to do, but I loved to play and I sure did hate it when I wasn't out there on the field.

Tech finished 9–1 that year, with our only loss a one-point defeat by Southern Mississippi on a field goal with 37 seconds to play. We seniors were proud of our record. We knew we had helped to bring Louisiana Tech football from 1–9 to 9–1, and we had a right to be proud.

Most of the guys never played football again. Tech was the end of the road for them, and they quit on a great, successful year.

For me, the fun had just begun. I was going to have to learn the pain of losing all over again, because I sure had plenty of it out there waiting for me!

8
Playing With the Big Boys

I HAD BEEN NAMED to some All-American teams my junior and senior years, and after the season ended in 1969 I got a chance to do something that I had dreamed about for years. I was invited to play for the Southern All-Stars in the North-South Shrine Game in Miami, Florida, and the Senior Bowl in Mobile, Alabama.

When I got those invitations, I didn't even hesitate before saying *yes.* I'll bet I was the most enthusiastic senior to report to camp in Miami. I had several reasons to be so gung-ho. First of all, this was my first chance to play with the "big boys." I was the kid from the little small-time college, remember? I was the kid who went to Tech because he was afraid to face big-league competition, remember? And now I was going to Miami and Mobile to see if I was good enough to do my stuff against the guys from the major universities. It still is a source of great irritation to me that, whenever a player from a so-called small college has a great year, everybody is eager to put his accomplishments down to mediocre competition. People never seem to want to give a guy credit for outstanding achievement on the football field unless he does it in the Southeastern Conference or the Big Eight Conference or some place like that.

I think that's a bum rap all the way. Lots of people will disagree with me on this, but I believe that Louisiana Tech my junior and senior years could have walked onto the field with any team in the country and played them even. I don't think the good athletes at a school like Alabama or Southern California are one bit better than the good athletes at schools like Louisiana Tech. It is simply a matter of the good schools having more money and the reputation that goes with being around for a long time. If you took a school like Tech those two years, put them on national TV and called them a major college, nobody could tell the difference between them and the big-name teams in the country. The big schools have more money and give more scholarships, so they get a larger number of the top high-school athletes. Except for that, there is very little difference—not nearly as much, I'll assure you, as the average football fan thinks.

Another reason that I was eager to play in Miami and Mobile that winter was because I was a sure-enough, old-fashioned supporter of the Deep South. I have always had a great sense of regional identity—even when I was a kid in Iowa, I felt like a Southerner. I have always loved the South and still do. So when I went to Miami I was eager to hit a lick for Dixie. And then there was a final source of motivation: The realization that all the pro scouts would be watching, and my position in the NFL draft would depend greatly on how I did in those All-Star games.

When I got to Miami, guess who was the head coach for the South? Bill Peterson, the coach from Florida State who had sent me packing three years earlier. And guess who he had with him? Bill Cappleman, his starting quarterback at FSU. I worked like a horse that week during practice, and felt like I had beaten Cappleman out and should start, but Peterson started his boy anyway. Well, that wasn't so bad because I figured I would get in to play about half the game anyway, but that's not the way it turned out. The game went on and on and we were losing and still Peterson stayed with Cappleman. I finally got in during the 4th quarter and did fairly well, but we lost and when I left Miami I was really upset.

Here I was trying to prove myself against the big-college players, and Peterson wouldn't even give me a chance to see what I could do. It wasn't fair. A similar situation occurred in 1972 at the College All-Star Game in Chicago. Pat Sullivan came to that game as the Heisman Trophy winner and had one of the best records in college ball. But the All-Star coach was Bob Devaney of Nebraska, and he had his quarterback, Jerry Tagge, with him. The All-Star team got clobbered all night long, their offense got nowhere, and still Devaney stayed with his boy while Sullivan sat on the bench. When he finally got to play in the fourth quarter, he led the team on a long drive for their only touchdown and won the Most-Valuable-Player Award.

Well, after that night in Miami, I forgot all about winning for the dear ol' South and went to Mobile with blood in my eye. I knew I was as good as the major-college quarterbacks; I had seen them throw; I had played with them; and I knew I was every bit as good. I went to Mobile determined to beat out the competition, start for the South, and prove that I could play with anybody.

Coach Don Shula of the Miami Dolphins was the head coach for the South team in the Senior Bowl, and playing for him that one week helps me to understand better why he is such an outstanding pro coach. He is the kind of guy that you enjoy playing for—somehow he knows the key to motivation, the ability to make players do what the coach wants—and like it. And he was completely fair. He gave everyone on the squad an even shot at starting, and I won the quarterback position.

For a while I was afraid I wouldn't even get into the game in the Senior Bowl. During a practice session in Miami, I had been running pass routes, just goofing off, and I had stepped into a little depression on the practice field. I went down like I was shot—a hamstring pull. It slowed me down some that week, but by the time I got to Mobile I thought the problem was gone. The first day of practice we were running timed 40-yard dashes so the coaches could check our speed. As I took off from the starting line to run my sprint I felt something pop behind my knee, and I knew the hamstring was gone again. I was scared to tell Coach Shula about it—afraid he wouldn't let me play on one bum leg. So all week I tried to hide it from him, and in the game itself I was so revved up I hardly even noticed it.

The game was a thriller—a wide-open offensive battle that had the crowd spellbound all the way through. The North quarterback was Dennis Shaw, now with the Buffalo Bills. I had the hot hand, threw a couple of touchdown passes, and we tied the game. I was named Most Valuable Player and left Mobile feeling like I had done what I came to do.

In the last few minutes of that game, I was passing from my own end zone. Just as I turned the ball loose, I got a vicious shot in the ribs from Wesley Grant, a UCLA lineman playing for the North. It hurt worse than any injury I'd ever had before, and when they taped me up on the sidelines I knew I was hurt. At the hospital they told me I had three broken ribs to go along with that hamstring pull, so I left the Senior Bowl as the Walking Wounded.

9
#1 Draft Choice

THE PLAYER DRAFT of the National Football League was only about a week after that game, and I knew I was going to be sitting pretty. As most football fans know, college players have no choice of professional teams to play for. The 26 teams in the NFL choose players in turns, the team with the poorest record picking first, the team with the next-worst record picking second, and so on until the Super Bowl winner chooses last. Then they start over again and go through the same process seventeen times, until the 442 best players in the country are chosen.

The pro teams naturally pour immense amounts of money and effort into the drafting process, since staying on top (or getting off the bottom) in the NFL depends on keeping the roster full of good, young players. For the college athlete, there is nothing to do but sit and wait. Whoever chooses him owns him, and that's all there is to it.

Naturally I was excited about the prospects of going high in the draft. An early choice usually means more money at contract time—as well as the honor of being that desirable to some pro team. The Pittsburgh Steelers and the Chicago Bears had finished the previous season with identical 1–13 won-lost records, and they flipped a coin to decide who had the right to made the first pick. Pittsburgh won.

On the morning that the draft was to begin, I was still asleep at my folks' home in Shreveport when the phone rang. Mom came to wake me up, telling me that it was a long-distance call from Pittsburgh. We thought we knew what the call must be, and my parents and brother huddled around me while I rubbed the sleep from my eyes and picked up the receiver.

We weren't wrong. The voice on the other end of the line belonged to Dan Rooney, vice-president of the Pittsburgh Steelers. He was crisp and cool and to the point. The Steelers were going to pick me first in the draft in about an hour, he said. And how did I feel about it, he wanted to know. Great, I said. Okay, they would be in touch, he said. End of conversation.

That phone call touched off a round of the kind of hugging and kissing and back-slapping that is our family style. Then I went to get my pajamas off and my clothes on before the newspaper and television people got to the house. They were all there about an hour later when the official call came from Pete Rozelle, informing me that I had been the #1 Draft Choice in the country. When the call came, my parents were in the living room entertaining the reporters, and I was out in the backyard throwing the football back and forth with my little brother Craig. Somehow it just seemed appropriate. Not only that, but he wanted somebody to play catch with him, and I was the only person available!

I had received a certain amount of attention from the news

media during my years at Tech, but nothing at all to prepare me for the massive influx of writers and photographers who set out to get my story after the draft. I was flying to various cities around the country, appearing at banquets in Miami, Los Angeles, and Chicago, and everywhere I went there were writers asking me all kinds of questions. I was having the time of my life and had never even thought about such things as "image" or "stereotype." When a reporter asked a question, I just let 'er rip—whatever came into my mind I said it. I was a babe in the woods, and the reporters were having a field day.

Throughout high school and college, my only contact with the press had been the Shreveport papers and broadcasting stations. They liked me and I liked them. When I played well, they bragged on me and when I didn't, they bragged on me anyway—or at least ignored me. And the fact that I was a slow-talking, churchgoing, country-music-loving Southern boy wasn't any novelty to them—the woods were full of guys just like me around Shreveport.

When the draft pick came, it was a different story. Boy, did I ever get my baptism of fire! I was new meat for those reporters: naïve, immature, shy, and—heaven forbid—completely candid. The angle was too good to pass up, I suppose, and before I knew what hit me I had been hung with a national image of a big, dumb, small-college, Southern, rural, Bible-totin' kid who had a strong arm and not enough sense to get in out of the rain. A hick, that's what they painted me as—a hick.

The lowest blow of all came from a writer from *Sports Illustrated* magazine. He came into Ruston a few days after the draft and interviewed me. *Nice guy,* I thought, and I did just like I thought I was supposed to do—acted natural and tried to be myself and answered his questions as honestly as I could.

When the magazine came out, there I was on the cover, big as Christmas. I was really pleased, but when I opened the magazine and began to read what that fellow had written, I got embarrassed—then got mad—then got embarrassed again. Here is part of the story:

> Pittsburgh has never seen the likes of Terry Bradshaw, the big blond quarterback from Louisiana Polytechnic Institute who was the first to go in last week's pro football draft. But then Terry Bradshaw has never seen the likes of Pittsburgh. In fact, until this year the only big city he had ever seen was New Orleans.
>
> . . . Sitting in the Ruston, La., Holiday Inn restaurant last Friday night, Terry Bradshaw got so excited at the prospect of playing for the Steelers he ordered another cup of coffee. "When they called me and told me they'd drafted me No. 1, I just couldn't believe it," he said. "I mean, all along I wanted to go with a loser. . . ."
>
> . . . Bradshaw can't wait to make his next move. "I just want to bust out and get started in pro ball," he says. "I've seen so much the past few weeks, going to Miami and L.A. and meeting people like Roman Gabriel, Joe Kapp and Carl

Eller, well, I can't wait to jump right in. Because if there's one thing I learned in Miami and L.A. it's that just because a guy has long hair doesn't mean he's a bad guy."

Come next July, Terry Bradshaw will toss Duchess [my white boxer] into the front seat of his new "Burgundy Fire" Thunderbird ("It's elite, but not *elite* elite"), and squeal off for the Steelers' camp. When he gets to Pittsburgh he might even lower his side-burns.

And a little later on, *Newsweek* did a cover story on me with the same angle:

He possesses the passing arm of a Joe Namath combined with the straight and narrow morals of a Southern Baptist. After only a few days in training camp, he became the acknowledged leader of the hitherto jaded Pittsburgh Steelers; yet he retains a refreshing, country-boy modesty and naïveté. . . .

. . . and one interviewer walked away from a chat with the ebullient rookie and quipped, "He reminds you of Jack Armstrong—on one of Jack's best days." (The 21-year-old Bradshaw asked, "Who's Jack Armstrong?")

". . . I'm a very emotional player," Bradshaw admits. "If someone's doing great, then I'm liable to hug him and kiss him and just go wild. That's just the way I am, I show my feelings. . . ."

Seasoned offensive linemen . . . didn't even flinch when the rookie subjected them to preachy little sermons such as, "I want you guys to forget all that old hogwash about your having a losing attitude. . . ."

. . . Whenever he flubbed he would berate himself with his own kind of four-letter words—"No, dang it, no"—and then solicit advice from the veterans; after successful plays he would howl with delight. . . .

You get the idea, I'm sure. The picture is plain as can be: Terry Bradshaw, bumpkin and overgrown kid. The Blond Bayou Bomber, fresh out of the sticks with a football under his arm and a crooked grin on his face. I have some friends who are writers, and they remind me that writers have to make a living too. They have to write something, and in my case the chance to draw a graphic, vivid picture of "Li'l Abner in a football uniform" (as one writer called me) was just too tempting. But here I was just a kid, not even out of college yet, and there were millions of people all over the country who had never met me and knew nothing about me, reading this junk and buying an image of me that was an inaccurate one.

There were three parts to The Image, really, and each was bothersome in a different way:

Image #1—Terry Bradshaw the Dummy. This was the most galling of all. Football players in general have trouble shaking the "dumb jock" stereotype—but to be labeled a dumb football player is double trouble. I'm no intellectual, but I'm certainly not unintelligent either. After all, I was a college senior—what was I supposed to be, Albert Einstein? I think a lot of this part of the image was generated strictly by the fact that I didn't play coy and cagey with interviewers. I just said what I thought, and they must have figured, *Hey, get a load of this kid. He's so dumb, he's telling the truth.* So the nicer I treated them, the less they thought I had on the ball.

Image #2—Terry Bradshaw the Rube. Okay, I wasn't the most cosmopolitan kid who ever stepped in front of a microphone, but did that mean I grew up in the backwoods? If I had "put on the dog" a little, played the big role, acted cool and cynical and worldly-wise, I would not have gotten the rap I did. But when I get excited, I don't mind acting excited; and if I love football and Mom and apple pie, I don't mind telling people that's what I like. Then, too, I think part of the rube image sprang from my style of expressions. I love to tell a good story, and use lots of expressions and phrases that don't sound exactly uptown to people who live outside my part of the country. Maybe I should be duller, and then people would think I'm from the city!

Image #3—Terry Bradshaw the Super Saint. I'm no Holy Joe—no super Christian who never does anything wrong. I never have claimed to be. But I *am* a Christian, and have never minded telling people that I am. So right away the press painted me as some kind of preacher—a kind of grid-iron Billy Graham. And the problem is that this particular part of the image I can't refute because if I do, the public misinterprets my disclaimer as a denial of my faith. I don't want that. I want to go on record as a believer. This particular point is so important to me, and so easily misunderstood, that it deserves a full explanation, and this is the place to make it.

10
A Christian—No Super Saint

I AM NOT a Super Saint. I am not even a minister. I am a Christian layman—plain and simple. I am a Christian because I believe Jesus Christ is the Son of God, and because I asked Him to forgive my sins and make me His child when I was a high-school student.

It would be nice if, because I am a football player, God would give me some kind of special spiritual something that would keep me from having the same problems and temptations that other Christians have. Some people seem to think that He does—or ought to. They act as if God is some kind of celestial Joe Fan—that He is just another part of the star-struck public that cherishes the myth that a football player is somehow a different kind of human being from the average person. That is, of course, not true at all. Pro athletes (or celebrities of any kind, for that matter) don't have an inside track with God. As far as God is concerned, they are just individuals, no more important—not even more interesting—than the neighborhood grocer. And so they work out their relationships with God in the same way that anyone else does. They have good and bad moments, experience moods that are alternately high and low, fail in some spiritual tasks and succeed in others.

And so I don't have any more of a monopoly on spiritual insight than any other layman does. But I do have my life to live, and I am trying to live it in a way that pleases God. And I also have a certain amount of influence that goes along with being in the public eye. That influence must be exerted in one direction or another, and I want mine to be spent in the support of things that are good and decent.

All my life I was taught to respect God and the church. My dad and mom were strict with us kids, and I always stayed so busy with sports that I never got into any of the trouble that lots of teen-agers get involved in these days. But I never really made a commitment to Christ in a personal way until late in my high-school years. I had been baptized in the Baptist church we attended but I had never become a Christian.

One Sunday night before service the youth minister at our church called me in and told me I ought to make a dedication to God so that I could use that influence for Him. When he first hit me with it, I about laughed in his face. Being a Christian and telling people about Jesus was the furthest thing from my mind—I didn't care about that stuff. But he continued to talk to me, and what he was saying began to sink in. He was a forceful guy, and by the time he asked me if I would pray with him, I was ready to pray. When I left that office I was crying and asking the Lord to enter my heart.

From that time on I spent lots of my weekends and summertime evenings speaking at churches and youth rallies. I learned to pray and found what a source of strength prayer could be. I started reading the Bible, and developed an interest in it that is still a strong part of my life. I really got into a deep religious thing, and felt a strong commitment toward the ministry. I thought about it and prayed about it and finally decided that what God wanted me to do was play football to the best of my ability and lend my influence as a football player to His cause.

I hope that was an honest decision, and didn't spring from my lack of courage to do what God wanted me to do. I know God calls football players to be ministers sometimes—like Bill Glass, for example—but I honestly believe that I made the right choice. It still bothers me sometimes—still talks to me, especially when things aren't going too well. I get tempted to say, *See, God wanted you to be a preacher, but you wouldn't, so now look what's happening.* But that is just a bit of spiritual immaturity, I think. I believe I'm doing what God wants me to do. The job is just to do it better—play football better and live for Him better.

As a student at Tech, I spent one summer in the closest thing to full-time ministry that I've ever done—working as a youth minister at a Methodist Church in Ruston. I directed the youth program for the summer, conducting the youth services, leading the singing, lining up speakers, teaching Sunday school—the whole works. It was a pretty typical job of that sort, I guess, with the older folks in the church—

especially the little old ladies—constantly disapproving of the trips and outings that I planned, just like little old ladies do in churches everywhere. They about drove me up the wall.

One thing was not typical, though, and that was where I lived. The church had a big, old, ramshackle, fifteen-room house, and put me there for the summer. It had apparently been a favorite stopping-off place for bums and derelicts, because burglars or bums or somebody broke into the place seven times during that summer. One night I was lying in bed when I had the feeling that someone was watching me. I went over to the window, opened the blinds, and was face-to-face with a big hulking man who was standing on a stool outside looking in the window. As soon as I opened the blinds, *Bam!* he hit me over the head with a Coke bottle and put my lights out.

Another time I saw a man standing in the hallway, and I chased him out of the hall and into the woods behind the house. A couple of weeks later a man came in a window in the hall and started trying to get into the room where I was sleeping. I jumped out the window, got in my car, went and picked up a buddy of mine. He took a big stick and headed around the house one way and I got a Coke bottle and went the other way. As we started creeping around the house, the bum inside stuck a gun out of a window and shot at us. Boy, talking about hauling it out of there—we did! We met way down the street and grabbed each other, scared to death. The police finally checked into the goings-on and found out that there had been a bunch of transients living in the attic all summer, apparently trying to scare me off. They succeeded. After that incident with the gun, I moved into another house and never went back.

I have always believed in God, have tried to live for Him since high school, and my faith in Him has been very meaningful to me ever since. But when I became a #1 Draft Choice, I got this image as such a great Christian that it became a real problem to me. I began to feel the pressure to live up to all the things that were written about me, and that is totally impossible. Writers and ministers—well meaning, I guess—would exaggerate some aspect of my religious life and then I foolishly felt like I had to live up to it.

A typical example: I read my Bible a lot in training camp because I have lots of time then. So the word gets out that I read my Bible every morning as soon as I get up. Period. So people write this in articles and introduce me to audiences by telling it—and it isn't true, literally speaking. I *don't* read my Bible every morning when I get up—I doubt if many Christians do. But if I say I don't in public, people get the idea that I am ashamed of the Bible or something—and that's not true either. On the other hand, if I sit still and listen to that said about me and don't correct it—I feel like a *hypocrite.*

Another example is the use of profanity. It is often written that I don't use bad language, and my teammates read that. But sometimes I slip, occasionally I fall back into those old habits, and swear on the ball field or somewhere where my teammates can hear, and they think, *Oh boy, there's that hypocrite Bradshaw again, acting so goody-goody to the public and cussing in the huddle.* And it's not a matter of being a hypocrite at all. It is just that football players make mistakes and fall short of their own standards sometimes just like anyone else does.

This matter of public exposure can really be a barrier to normal Christian growth. It has a tendency to rob a person of the opportunity to mature and develop as a Christian in a natural way. He is expected to be a saint overnight and never have a moment of weakness, or people will accuse him of being insincere all along. The expression of honest doubts and the struggle to resolve them, for example, is a part of every Christian's spiritual growth. The plumber who sits next to you in the pew can express his doubts and nobody raises an eye. But if a person in the public eye has doubts, he has to grapple with them alone, or certainly be very careful to whom he expresses them, for fear of being misquoted and represented as a "backslider" to the whole country.

The whole Super-Christian Image that I acquired when I first went to Pittsburgh was a bad deal. It was bad for my own personal Christian growth, and I had to struggle to keep it from snuffing out the really genuine commitment that I had made to God.

I once read a statement by Billy Casper, the great pro golfer, about his own Christian life that really struck a responsive chord. He said: "I think too much has been said and written about my religious life without people taking the time really to understand what it means in my life."

I'll say, *Amen!* to that and make it two, brother.

Although he served as batboy for his father's industrial league softball team as a grammar-schooler in Iowa, Terry Bradshaw's first and lasting love was football. *Left:* Terry wore the now-famed #12 in high school, then in college, and requested that number when he joined the Steelers. This is a flattopped Terry at Woodlawn High School in Shreveport, Louisiana. (Photo by Cowen, Shreveport, La.)

Few of his fans know that Bradshaw was a national champion javelin thrower while in high school. In fact, he received more than two hundred scholarship offers from colleges throughout the country to throw the javelin but he never seriously considered anything but football. (Shreveport *Times* Staff Photo) *Below:* It was a proud and happy moment for the Bradshaw family when Terry accepted the college scholarship from Louisiana Tech. That's his mom and dad seated next to him, while standing (left) is an assistant coach from Tech and (right) Lee Hedges, Woodlawn High School's head coach. (Shreveport *Times* Staff Photo)

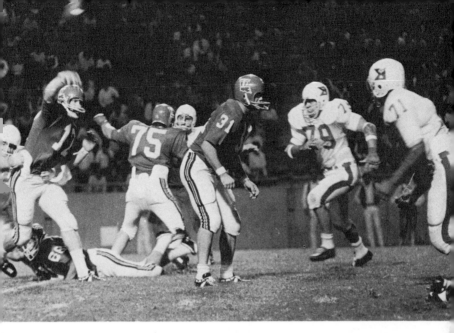

The Blond Bomber from Louisiana Tech unleashes one in a typical Bradshaw-to-Spinks pass during their junior year of college. *Below:* Don Shula, coach of the Miami Dolphins, poses with Terry before the Senior Bowl game in Mobile, Alabama, in 1969. Bradshaw started for the South in the game and was named Most Valuable Player.

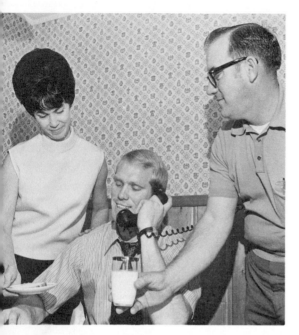

The nation's #1 Draft Ch○
takes an early morning
from Pittsburgh Steeler Vi
President Dan Rooney wh
his parents keep up his stren
with some breakfast. (Shre
port *Times* Staff Photo). *Bel*
With the Great City of Pi
burgh as a backdrop, I
Rooney and the new Steeler
in a restaurant for Terry's f
visit to town to meet the pr
and team brass.

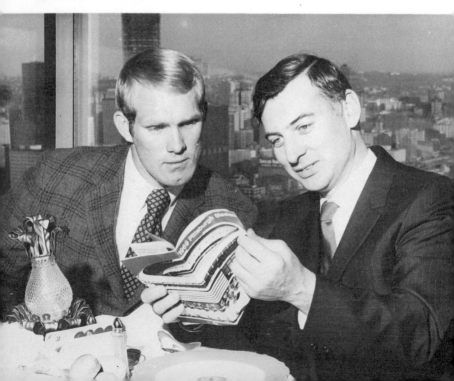

Mrs. Bradshaw visits her son in Divine Providence Hospital where he recuperates from surgery to remove calcium deposits in his thigh. This was in May before his rookie season. *Below:* After he was named #1 Draft Choice, Terry was invited to the White House to meet the nation's #1 Football Fan. (Official White House Photograph)

Oh, that wonderful first pres
son! Touchdown! *Below:* T
young quarterback ruefully
mits that he always said exac
what he thought in those ea
interviews with the press.
came out sounding like "A I
Abner in a football uniform

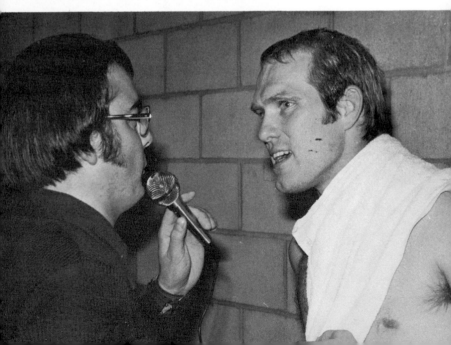

This is probably one of the most famous photographs of Terry Bradshaw. It appeared on the front page of a Pittsburgh paper the day after the game. Terry had time to blow bubbles because he was benched for the entire four quarters. *Below:* Defensive tackle Diron Talbert of the Washington Redskins bears down on #12 who looks anxiously for a receiver.

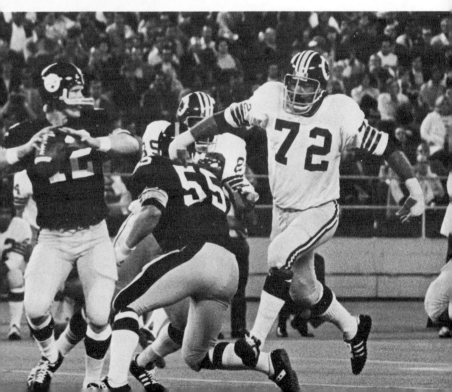

"The most painful injury I've ever had in football." That's how Terry described the dislocated finger injury he received in Oilers game. Here he nurses the sore hand while rookie quarterback Joe Gilliam gets ready to go in for him.

"A quarterback lives or dies by the skill of his offensive line—no matter how gifted he is." This photo shows what Bradshaw meant as the young and tough linemen prepare to "blow a hole in the defense big enough to drive a cement truck through." *Below:* Terry Bradshaw signs autographs for young admirers at the Steelers' training camp on the campus of St. Vincent's College in Latrobe, Pennsylvania.

Bradshaw uncorks a screen p
against the Colts at Baltimo
Colts' defensive end Bi
Newsome looks for the int
ception. *Below:* #12 can run
well as pass, as he does here
a tough game against the
Louis Cardinals. Big center R
Mansfield tries to clear aw
some of the opposition for hi

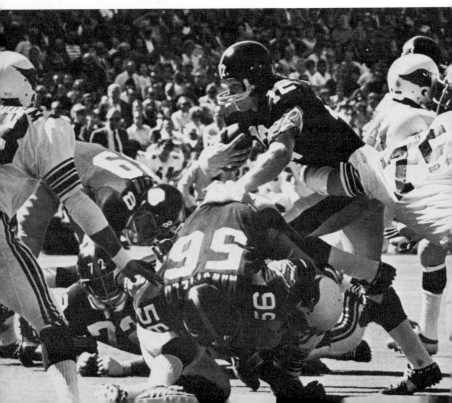

This Oakland Raider will have to run faster to catch up to the speedy quarterback before an enthusiastic Pittsburgh hometown crowd. After forty years —a winner at last. *Below:* Called the Miracle of Pittsburgh, this is the crazy play which took the first round in the playoffs by Pittsburgh's first division champs in history. Rookie back Franco Harris grabbed the ball when it popped free from the receiver and here he is running into the end zone with only seconds remaining on the clock.

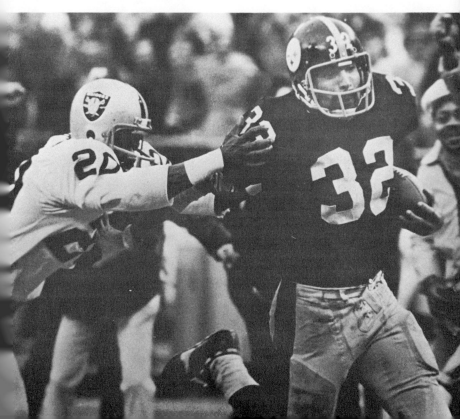

Mrs. Terry Bradshaw, the former Melissa Babish, native of Pittsburgh. As a former Miss Teenage America, Missy had been up the celebrity trail herself and was unimpressed by the fact that Terry was a pro-football player. They were married in February, 1972. [Photo by permission of Management: IFA/Concert Associates. Telephone: 213–556–1200.]

11
Temporary Toast of Pittsburgh

FOR THE NEXT few months, I was the toast of Pittsburgh. The papers smothered me with good ink, the fans seemed glad to see me coming to town, and the Steelers gave me the royal treatment.

Soon after the draft, I flew up to Pittsburgh to meet Art Rooney, the owner, and Chuck Noll, head coach, and meet the Pittsburgh media in a press conference. Everybody was just super, and I was eager to sign and get on with it. On the next trip up I took my father and a Shreveport attorney, Bob Pugh, along to begin the negotiations. We made an offer and they made an offer and we met somewhere in the middle. It was really that simple. I felt like I got what I was worth, and apparently the Steelers felt like I hadn't exactly stuck a gun to their heads, so things went smoothly.

The actual signing took place in the middle of the field at Three Rivers Stadium, the new home for the Steelers and the baseball Pirates which was still under construction. We had a little ceremony at a folding table placed on the raw dirt at the spot where the 50-yard line would be when the stadium was finished. There were workmen scattered all over the upper reaches of the stadium and they applauded when I walked out across the field for the signing.

When I signed that contract, I became the property of the Pittsburgh Steelers, and they gave me the old physical once-over and found that a calcium deposit had formed in my right thigh as an aftereffect of the hamstring muscle pull that I had suffered in the post-season games in Miami and Mobile. I went into Divine Providence Hospital in Pittsburgh in late May and had the deposit removed in surgery by Dr. John Best, the Steeler team doctor. I was glad that the deposit had been found before the year started, but the surgery kept me from working out in the week-long rookie camp that was held the first week in June, and that was a big disappointment.

The surgery caused another problem before it was all over, though—this time of an indirect nature. I had been scheduled to play in the Coaches All-American game in Lubbock, Texas, in late June, but had not recovered enough by then to play. But when the practice sessions started for the College All-Star game in Chicago in late July, I felt 100 percent and reported to camp. In the first workout, my legs felt a little sore, but not unusually so for an early practice like that. But then on the second day, I faked a handoff and started to roll out to my right when I felt a thigh muscle pop and I knew I had pulled it. I hobbled over to the sidelines and, soon afterwards, went in to shower and dress.

The Steelers had been worried about my trying to come back from the minor surgery too soon, and had asked Joe

Krupa, a former Steeler player living in Chicago, to keep up with my condition in the All-Star camp. He made a quick call to Pittsburgh, and the fat was in the fire. The Steelers didn't want me to play in the All-Star game, naturally, since they didn't want me to take a chance on getting hurt, and since the time I spent there would keep me out of their own preseason training camp. The pulled muscle was all the excuse they needed.

The officials of the College All-Star game, on the other hand, *did* want me to play, and in the worst way. They depended on having the well-known college players in the game to draw a crowd and attract TV interest. As the #1 Draft Choice and a flashy, passing quarterback, I was one of their biggest drawing cards. So they were determined that if I were healthy enough to play, I was going to play—and my NFL contract gave them the right to demand it of me. So it became a battle between the two doctors. First, the All-Stars had their doctor examine me. Predictably, he said that all I had was a muscle "twitch" and there was nothing wrong with me. "Play," he said. Then the Steelers flew me back to Pittsburgh where Dr. Best examined me and diagnosed my problem as a muscle pull—too severe to run on. "Don't play," he said. So there I stood, right in the middle. I really wanted to play in the game, but I didn't want to mess up my leg for good. So I did what the Steelers wanted—I pulled out of the game and came back to Pittsburgh.

George Strickler, director of the game, screamed and hollered. He accused the Steelers of babying me, of tricking the

All-Star officials, and of casting aspersions on the skill of his doctors. He threatened to appeal the matter to NFL Commissioner Pete Rozelle but mostly he just cried a lot. And me —I hobbled right into the Steelers' training camp on my bad leg. It was the first time I had ever been controversial—but it wasn't going to be the last!

The Steelers' training camp is held on the campus of St. Vincent College in Latrobe, Pennsylvania, a little town east of Pittsburgh. My rookie training was not a typical one. It came in the year of the NFL players' strike, and we rookies were in camp alone for the first few weeks. It was a hot, hot July, and that training camp, as all others, was sweltering and sweaty. I went into camp eager to play football. I had waited all winter and spring, and I was really ready to go. The offensive system that Coach Noll introduced me to when I arrived was the most complicated thing I had ever seen, and I worked hard at learning its ins and outs during that camp. The strike really helped. By the time the veterans came to camp we had already gone through half the playbook and I was beginning to catch on.

The other rookies hadn't paid much attention to all my press clippings in those first several days in camp, but when the veterans arrived they really laid it on me good. The training camp tradition includes lots of razzing of rookies by the veterans, and high-draft choices are usually singled out for the special treatment. There was one guy who gave me a rough time from the start—receiver Roy Jefferson. All the rookies feared him because he was such a big-mouth, always giving us a rough time. I remember the first day he came into camp. He burst into the dorm yelling, "Bradshaw, Bradshaw, where's that hot-shot Bradshaw?" He had everybody in the dorm looking for me, and I was scared to come out of my room.

That night (and practically every night afterwards), the tables were cleared after supper and the rookies had to get up and sing for the vets, appearing in order of their draft number. I belted it out that night: "Old Billy Goat was feelin' fine, ate three red shirts from off the line. . . ." The veterans booed me, threw jello at me, and I just stood up there smiling bigger than Dallas, man, singing that song. All the tomfoolery gets old pretty quickly, though, and with the strike behind us we had an unusually businesslike camp.

Now that I've had a couple of training camps behind me, I understand better why the vets pick on the rookies the way they do. It is purely to ease the tension of the camp and help the rookies—strange as it sounds—to fit in a little more easily. I can just about look at rookies now and tell whether they're going to make it or not; and if I figure they are not going to make it, I leave them alone. I guess if a rookie is really being pestered by the veterans, he ought to take it as a good sign.

The bravest (or craziest!) rookie I've ever seen was a tight end from the University of Georgia named Dennis Hughes. He would argue with the veterans, talk back to them, holler at them during practice. He was a real pistol. Another rookie was virtually the opposite of Hughes. He just couldn't get up the nerve to sing. I believe he would have preferred being cut to having to sing, so the vets didn't push him into it.

The first preseason game was to be in Jacksonville against the Miami Dolphins, and as it approached I became less carefree and thought more and more about what I was up against in Pittsburgh. This was a city that had fielded an NFL football team for thirty-seven years—since the founding of the league—and had never had a team earn a spot in the league playoffs. That would be enough to make the most patient fans in the world belligerent. You've heard the old saying, "Hell hath no fury like a woman scorned"? Well, even a woman scorned hath no fury like an NFL city with thirty-seven years and no division championship! Pittsburgh was ready for a winner—or else!

Not only had there been no championship in thirty-seven years, but the team had a recent history of "blowing the draft"—of taking chances on long-shot college players who never seemed to pan out—so the team never got any better. After all that time, the Steelers had managed only one victory in the previous season. When it was announced that the Steelers had used their number one choice to get me, I'm sure groans of dismay could be heard all over Pittsburgh. Like, "Oh, no, here we go again, wasting our draft pick on some guy from a place called *Louisiana Tech!*"

Then there was another item that increased the pressure: Pittsburgh already had a promising young quarterback. He was Terry Hanratty, a native of Western Pennsylvania and an extremely popular player locally. He had been a second-round draft choice only a year earlier, and had been a two-time All-American at Notre Dame, with a fabulous, record-setting career there. And this was to be the Other Guy—the quarterback whom I would have to fight for the starting job. The national press was already touting the battle for the starting job as a major clash before Hanratty and I had even met. We were cast in the roles of rivals from the very first, and he was a tough one to have to compete against.

When we walked out on the field for that first exhibition game against Miami, I was nervous as a cat. I didn't get into the game until the second half, and played fairly well when I got started. We lost that game, but at least I had gotten my feet wet and hadn't embarrassed myself.

After that first exhibition game, things seemed to click for me beyond what I had ever dreamed possible. I started the next preseason game against the big, bad Minnesota Vikings, and we beat them in Minnesota. We went two weeks without a game, then opened the new stadium in an exhibition game against the New York Giants. And—what do you know?—we beat *them*, too. Unbelieveable. The next preseason skirmish was against the Boston Patriots, and it had been conveniently scheduled for Shreveport, Louisiana. It was just like Old Home Folks Week down there: everybody and his dog came to see the Blond Bayou Bomber as a pro. It was terribly hot that night, and the grass was so high you could hardly pick your legs up. I almost passed out just warming up, it was so hot. But we really bombed Boston, scoring 31 points on them to the delight of the Shreveport crowd. "Hey, what is this?" people in Pittsburgh began to say, "Three preseason victories in a row? 31 points in a game? Where did you say that fellow Bradshaw was from again?"

The final exhibition game was against the Oakland Raiders on the West Coast. We killed them, 20 to 6. It seemed like everything I did was right. I had an 87-yard touchdown run called back on a penalty, and was feeling so good I didn't even mind. It was Magic Wand Time, and I was really riding high. We finished the preseason schedule with a 4–1 record, and I had completed 51 percent of my passes for 603 yards in 5 games. I was beginning to think pro ball was a piece of cake. I had made it big and there was nothing to do now but become a superstar.

I should have known better. And the fans who were getting football fever and lining up to buy tickets and thinking about a championship should have known better. And the overenthusiastic sportswriter who wrote, "Bring on the Super Bowl!" should have known better. But we didn't. We were all too hungry to win, and we forgot that they don't start counting them until the season begins. There was one note of caution in the otherwise reckless tone of the sports pages that week. A columnist making his weekly predictions wrote: "The Steelers? They'll lose to the Houston Oilers. You know they start playing for keeps this week." So dry. So cynical. *And so true.*

The Houston Oilers—everybody's favorite doormat—was to be the fodder for our Pittsburgh powerhouse in the first game. And when I woke up on the morning of the season opener, I actually *felt* the difference. I sensed a new kind of pressure, a whole different feeling from that tension of the preseason games. Things had changed now, and I could actually *feel* the difference on the day the regular season began. When I went out to warm up for the Houston game, I really felt strange. I had an exhausted feeling, an empty feeling—there was just a big nothing there where my competitive instinct should have been. I had no feeling whatsoever for the game. I guess I was scared—scared of doing badly or losing or something.

On the first play from scrimmage I called a pass, my receivers were covered, so I ran it up the middle and got clobbered. That set the pattern for the whole day. Later I threw a 70-yard pass to Hubie Bryant which just slithered off his hands into the end zone. I underthrew a receiver who was wide open and could have scored. I stunk. So in the 4th quarter Coach Noll pulled me and put Hanratty in. He threw a touchdown pass right off the bat, and I about died. That sounds selfish and stupid—but it's true. I was so upset about being pulled, so miserable that I had played so poorly that I felt like crying right there on the bench. I felt like it was up to me to deliver that game to the people of Pittsburgh and I was crushed that I had failed so miserably. We lost the game 19–7, and I had gone 4 of 16 in the passing department. After the game I cancelled a postgame radio interview that had been scheduled, then felt bad about it and did it anyway. Then I went back to the locker room and cried in the shower. I stayed around the locker room a long time that evening, went back home to my apartment, cooked myself some dinner, and went to bed. I was sick, and I tossed and turned until the early morning hours.

That next Tuesday I went back to the stadium for practice, and the only thing on my mind was that I had lost my starting job. Coach Noll was not too rough on me, and the axe that I expected to fall never fell. "Don't worry," he told me, "you're still my quarterback. Let's get to work and see if we can get some offense going." I felt better already.

The next week we faced Denver on the road. I got off to a better start in that game, but early in the second half I got my bell rung. I was scrambling when Dave Costa got me right across the head with his forearm and wiped me out. Hanratty came in and got hurt himself, and we wound up losing the game 16–13. We drove all the way down to their 27-yard line with 1:52 left on the clock and Gene Mingo, our kicker, missed a field goal that would have tied it. I had directed the drive, and never doubted that Mingo could kick the field goal until it sailed wide.

In that game I got my first look at Chuck Noll when he was angry. I don't mean displeased—I mean flat-out mad! A few of the guys were goofing off in the half-time locker-room meeting, not paying attention, and he jumped on them like a chicken on a june bug. Man, the coaches never talked that way at Louisiana Tech. It made an impression on me— scared me to death—and you'd better believe I've listened to every word he has ever said to me since then.

We were 0–2, but I felt a bit better as we prepared for the

third game of the season against archrival Cleveland. We were on the road this week, and the crowd at the Cleveland stadium was the largest I had ever seen—over eighty thousand fans present. I was awestruck by that crowd. The game started with a big break for us. Cleveland fumbled the opening kickoff and we took the ball, marched it down to their 7-yard line, and Mingo came in and missed another field goal. So much for the big break.

In that Cleveland game I was nailed for a safety—the *third* time in three games. I dropped back to pass, the defensive line came in on me, and instead of unloading the ball, I let them box me in and dump me in the end zone. I was learning fast that the pro linemen were bigger and faster and tougher to elude than college linemen. Against Cleveland I was dumped behind the line of scrimmage *seven* times.

The hero of that game was a rookie quarterback, all right —but it wasn't me. Mike Phipps, who had been taken third in the NFL draft from Purdue, came off the bench in the second half in his first pro appearance ever. It was a doozy! The Browns trailed 7–2, and were on their own 10-yard line. Phipps promptly led them 90 yards for a TD to put them ahead 9–7. Three plays later one of their cornerbacks picked off one of my passes and returned it 38 yards to score. Just like that—we had gone from up 7–2 to down 15–7, and that was the old ball game. It was a bitter, disappointing loss to a team we really wanted to beat.

12
From Bad to Worse

JUST WHEN IT seemed that we would never win, the Buffalo Bills came to town. During the game, Coach Noll alternated between Hanratty and me, and the system seemed to work. We won the game 23–10 and there was joy in Pittsburgh. But there wasn't very much joy in my apartment that night because (happy as I was finally to put a win under our belt) I had to face up to the fact that I had lost my grip on the starting quarterback job, and on the leadership of the team. I had it in my hands and had let it slip away, and nobody knew that better than I did.

The magic that we had felt during that terrific preseason was gone—all drifted away to who-knows-where, and now all the anxiety and uncertainty was back again. I could tell it in the way the veterans acted toward me. During the preseason they had started to believe my press clippings. They had developed confidence that I *was* a winner, that I *was* good enough to take command of the ball team and lead it to a championship. I *had* had their confidence but I had wrecked it with too many incomplete passes and wild scrambles and wrong calls at the wrong time. And now I was in a fight for my starting job, and there was nothing I could do but hang on and hope things got better.

When I showed up for Tuesday's practice, all those fears were confirmed. Coach Noll announced in our weekly quarterback meeting that he was going to a system of alternating quarterbacks. Neither Hanratty nor I were to be number one but would divide the playing time in each game. Later in the day he made the same announcement to the press. They asked if the decision was due to Hanratty's good performance against Denver. "Bradshaw appears to have reached a plateau in his development, and he's become a little hesitant," Noll told them. (Translated, that means that I had started well but wasn't hacking it anymore, and was beginning to choke.)

That was Black Tuesday for me. To understand just how low that blow laid me, one must understand my attitude toward individual leadership on a football team. I believe that a team—to play consistent, winning football—must have a leader. I mean a single, on-the-field leader who holds things together and keeps the team going over the rough spots. That leader is the quarterback, and it is foolish to expect that kind of leadership from two different guys who are shuttling in and out of the game. A two-quarterback system is bad for everybody: bad for the team because they never know who's in charge; bad for the quarterbacks because they are always under pressure to outperform the other guy; bad for the coach because he is always being second-guessed about which one should be in the game at a given time. I just don't think it works—and anytime a team wins with a two-quarterback system I think it is in *spite* of the system, and not because of it.

In my case it was doubly bad because I felt like I had let my teammates down. I had come in with all those great promises, and the veterans on the team had treated me just super. When we hit that preseason win streak, they accepted me as their quarterback and were looking to me to keep performing and lead them to a good season. Now the dream world was collapsing. I wasn't leading anyone anywhere. And I could almost see the looks on their faces saying, *Man, we really got took in. He had us believing he was something special and it turns out he's just another erratic rookie.*

And to make it worse, our next game was in the Houston Astrodome against the Oilers, and all my family was planning to be there from Shreveport, and my girl friend was coming down from Odessa, Texas. I was supposed to be coming into Houston as a conquering hero, but it surely hadn't been working out that way. I met my folks and our whole entourage went out to dinner that night before the game. Then I went to bed early and got a good night's sleep. The next morning I ran into a pro scout in the motel lobby whom I hadn't seen since the year before when he was scouting me at Tech. Well, this fellow wanted to talk, and I just couldn't get away from him. Finally, I got loose from the guy and walked into the dining room—fifteen minutes late. On a pro football team, there is nothing minor about being late to anything so I was hit with a routine fine for my tardiness.

The game was one of the roughest I've ever played in. The Houston defense was big and mean and they hit like a bunch of Mack trucks. One of their linebackers, Ron Pritchard, spent half the afternoon sitting on my head. Three times he came right through the line without being touched and sacked me before I could get rid of the ball. It was that kind of tough defensive battle on both sides. Oiler quarterback Charley Johnson had his collarbone broken and went out for the day.

Late in the second quarter I finally threw one for all the money—my first TD pass in the pros. We were on our own 33-yard line, trailing 3-0, going nowhere. I hit Ron Shanklin, another rookie, with a hard, high shot just as he crossed midfield. Leroy Mitchell, the Oiler cornerback who was covering him, fell as he leaped to deflect the ball and Shanklin turned on the speed and scored untouched. That touchdown was a sweet one, and it was good enough to win the game 7-3. I had a pretty good day, completing 8 of 17 for 208 yards, and most of all, had put another game in the victory column.

I couldn't stand the prosperity. Before I ever strapped my helmet on again, I was already in the doghouse.

My parents had been at the game, remember, and after it was over I got permission to return to Shreveport with them. No sweat, Noll said, just be at the team meeting on Tuesday morning as usual. So off I went to Shreveport. I had scheduled a late Monday night flight to Pittsburgh that would get me there in time for the meeting. But the airport got fogged in—a real freak for Shreveport—and they called me from the airlines at about 10:30 Monday night to tell me my plane had been delayed. I waited around (hoping the fog would lift) for a couple of hours, then they cancelled the flight.

So I called Coach Noll. He hit the ceiling. Coach Noll is a gentleman, you understand, and I had gotten him out of bed in the middle of the night, so he didn't scream and holler or anything. He was calm and unruffled, but I could tell that he was really teed off. I told him my sad story. "Well, Terrence," he said (he always called me Terrence when he was mad at me that rookie year), "what time will you get in, Terrence?"

"It looks like about 1:00 or 1:30 tomorrow afternoon, Coach."

"Well, Terrence, you know it is the duty of a player to get back in time for the Tuesday meeting when he doesn't return with the team. That is at 11:00 tomorrow, Terrence."

"Yessir, Coach, but there's nothing I can do about it. The weather's really bad here, and no planes are leaving."

"Well, Terrence, you be sure to come by my office as soon as you get into town, Terrence."

"Yessir, Coach. I sure will, Coach."

My flight finally took off from Shreveport, but it couldn't land in Pittsburgh, was diverted to St. Louis, and I had to call Coach Noll again from St. Louis to tell him that I not only had missed the team meeting, but would miss practice and the quarterback meeting that afternoon as well. I finally arrived in Pittsburgh late Tuesday night, knowing I was in hot water.

The next morning I got up very early and drove to the Steelers' offices. I got there before anyone—secretaries, receptionist, coaches, anyone. I was scared and nervous and felt as guilty as an old egg-sucking dog. Finally Noll came in and called me into his office.

He let me have it right between the eyes. I had been irresponsible and undependable, he said. I had been foolish to schedule such a late flight into Pittsburgh—even if I had made it I would have been exhausted from flying all night, he said. I had let the team down because we had a big game coming up, he said. He would have to make an example out of me, and he was fining me three hundred dollars, and I would have to return to Pittsburgh with the team after all future road games, he said.

Yessir, I said, and crawled out. He was right, and I was rookie-wrong, and I knew it, and that was all there was to it. The incident never came up again between us.

That week I got my first taste of being Peck's Bad Boy in the newspapers. Some of the local sportswriters were running out of patience with me anyway. They had treated me like the Salvation of the Steelers when I came. No rookie was ever treated better by the press than I was during that preseason and early season in Pittsburgh. But after those opening three losses and my spotty performance in the regular season, things were beginning to go sour. I began to be called a "troubled rookie," and some of the writers started backing off their early enthusiasm for me.

When the story of the fine broke, the papers squeezed it

for all it was worth. That afternoon there was a six-column banner headline across the top of the sports page: BRAD-SHAW MISSES PRACTICE, FINED, and underneath, NOLL UP-SET, VISIBLY ANGERED BY ROOKIE'S ABSENCE. The story pointed out that I had cost the team a day's work in preparation for the game next week against the Raiders in Oakland. I decided that the only way to show that I hadn't hurt the team with my absence was to go out to Oakland and beat the Raiders that Sunday.

We got thrashed, 31–14. Offensively, we just couldn't get anything going. I was hitting my receivers pretty well, but every time we started to move the ball I would cut a bad one loose and it would be intercepted to kill our drive. I threw 4 interceptions in the game, and was caught and dumped several times when I tried to scramble out of the pocket to look for my receivers. Hanratty and I divided the quarter-back time again, and he didn't play much better.

The Raiders jumped all over us early, and were ahead 24–7 at half time. We never got into the ball game. Daryle Lamonica, their quarterback, was injured early and the Old Man, George Blanda, came in and picked our defense to pieces. He threw 3 TD passes of 44, 19, and 43 yards, and their rookie receiver Ray Chester (from Morgan State) caught 3 TD passes to be the two heroes for the day.

Well, we were 2–4 now and had one of the most important games of the year coming up. We were to play the Cincinnati Bengals at home on national Monday-night television. It was the first year of the Monday-night-pro-football telecasts, and commentators Howard Cosell and Don Meredith were all the rage. The viewing audience would be enormous, and it would be my first time on national TV as a pro. More importantly, if we were to have a chance to get back into the race for the division title, we had to beat Cincinnati, since they were in the same division with us. Lo and behold, Coach Noll announced that I would be starting the game. This was the chance I was waiting for. A really super game here and I felt like I could nail down the #1 quarterback spot again.

I was "up" for that Bengal game more than I had been in several weeks. The adrenalin was really flowing. Down on the field before game time I saw Howard Cosell standing with a microphone in his hand. He called me over and said he wanted to introduce me to the television audience, so I stood there with him for a minute.

He looked out in front of him in his best TV style and spoke into the microphone in that pompous way of his: "And now. Ladies and gentlemen. Let me introduce to you. The National Football League's #1 *flop,* quarterback Terry Bradshaw."

That embarrassed me so badly, I just stood with my mouth hanging open, a big blush spreading over my face. Then Cosell turned to me, laughed, and told me it was all a joke —that we were not on the air and his microphone was dead. Just a little joke, he said. I didn't think it was so funny.

The game began and, to make a long story short, I blew my big chance. The Cincinnati defense was not playing well that night. They were below par for some reason, and I could sense that they could be had, but I was unable to move the ball. I played terribly, missing receivers in the open field, reacting to defensive shifts hesitantly and uncertainly. I looked bad—I *was* bad. At half time I had missed a handful of scoring opportunities, had completed only 4 of 12 passes for a pitiful 40 yards, and we were behind on the scoreboard 10–7.

Even after such a horrible first half, Coach Noll decided to stick with me, and I started the 3rd quarter. His patience didn't last long. Early in that quarter I threw the ball into the turf on a 3rd-and-10 play, and Noll told Hanratty to get loosened up. I was standing on the sidelines, my head bowed, when he got up behind our bench and started to warm up and the crowd on that side of the field let out a big cheer. Noll was putting that bum Bradshaw on the bench, and the fans were happy.

Hanratty came in on the next series of downs, moved the team, and saved the day for us. Trailing 10–7 in the fourth quarter, Hanratty wound up and fired a 72-yard TD pass to rookie receiver Dennis Hughes. It was an unusual play. Hughes was supposed to run a short hook pattern, but he didn't—instead blew right past Bengal defender Kenny Graham. It was a busted play, but to the fans in the stadium and on TV it looked like it was planned all the way. After Hughes caught the ball, Graham also caught up to him, and Hughes stuck out his hand to stiff-arm him. That cornerback somehow got Hughes' finger in his mouth as he went by and clamped down on it hard. He came to the sidelines with his finger bleeding. He told the reporters after the game, "I would have bit him back but I've got eight teeth missing." That Dennis Hughes was some character!

Hanratty came right back after that play and directed a 52-yard drive for another touchdown. He looked great, threw 7 of 11 for 128 yards, and we won the game 23–10 and moved back into contention for the division championship.

So I should have been happy—right? We won a big game and I should have been happy and I should have told the reporters that it didn't matter to me who played so long as we won. But I wasn't happy. I had played lousy on national TV and been benched. Hanratty had nailed down the starting quarterback job with a great performance. And I was really feeling low. So when the reporters came around after the game, I told them exactly how I felt—and that was the biggest mistake of my life.

It was a hairy night in the dressing room. My locker stall and Hanratty's were side by side. He was in high spirits (naturally) and was accepting congratulations from everybody. And there I was in the next stall, dejected and blue, more upset than I had been all year. The reporters had a great time. They asked me if I thought Hanratty should be the starting quarterback now. "Sure," I said, "it's obvious; he's earned it; every time he comes in he does a great job." They asked Noll the same question and he said, "I don't know. I'll have to make that decision after I see the films." Standard coach's reply, but the handwriting was on the wall.

I felt terrible, so I just let all my frustration hang out that night. "If that's the way it's going to be," I said, "then I want to be traded. I don't want to sit on the bench and I'm not going to—not here anyway. I guess it sounds bad, but if I play second-string I'll play second-string behind a veteran." I continued, "Sure, I'm unhappy, and I don't mind admitting it. When I play bad football I don't care if the team wins 70–0 —I'm still unhappy. I'm dejected because I like people to be happy with me, and they aren't, and it is strictly my fault."

The next day every word of that insane outburst—and more—adorned the sports pages. I read it and just groaned. There was no way anyone would read that and understand how I felt. It sounded immature and selfish. I didn't know yet not to spill my emotions to sportswriters. I didn't know yet what power they held over public opinion. Mostly I didn't know that a fellow could make life miserable for himself by popping off at the wrong time like that.

It wasn't that I disliked Terry Hanratty or wished him ill. He was (and is) a nice guy and we got along well personally. But as far as I'm concerned being #1 ought to be the goal of every ballplayer, and anyone who is satisfied to play second-string deserves just that. I want to play first-string or not at all, and I think that competitive drive has put me where I am. Lots of people don't understand that, and they didn't then. They think that such an attitude makes me a "poor team man" or something. I can't help it. That's the way I feel. My only regret is that I didn't keep the feeling to myself!

That week was really the low-water mark of the year for me. On Tuesday afternoon Coach Noll called to tell me not to be too upset, and not to talk to any reporters about the quarterbacking situation. That was good advice, but it came too late. A writer had already been out to see me that morning and I had vented my spleen to him. By then I was feeling sorry for myself, and I told the writer that I was going to retire from football and become a Baptist minister. I was so low I was just saying anything—whatever came to mind. Noll read that story (after he had asked me to keep quiet), and I was farther back in the doghouse than ever.

The "Baptist minister" announcement wasn't entirely a ruse. I never actually decided to do that, but it *was* true that I had been seriously considering the ministry for the past couple of weeks. Since my teen-age years I had felt an inclination in that direction, and now that things were going sour, I was tempted to bail out and head for the pulpit. It was more than the pressure of football that was getting me down. Life was coming generally unglued. I had a girl friend back in Texas, and she was giving me a hard time. It was difficult for me to adjust to living alone in the big city of Pittsburgh after growing up with such close family ties. I was having trouble living the kind of Christian life that I expected of myself— and that bothered me constantly. Most of all, I was lonely and felt like one huge failure.

Most people in situations that are totally bleak turn to whatever really means the most to them—and I turned to seeking God and His will for me. That is not as easy for a celebrity as it is for the average person. I couldn't walk into a Baptist church there in Pittsburgh and go forward when

the altar appeal was made and rededicate myself to Christ.
I had been getting so much publicity about being such a good
Christian that it would have been a major incident for me to
do that. I was recognized everywhere I went. I longed for a
little anonymity for just one night, so I could slip into a little
church somewhere and go down to the altar and pray without causing a stir—but that was impossible.

So I had to fight my battles with myself, and make my
peace with the Lord, all alone in my apartment by myself.
I came in night after night wishing the whole season were
over and done with and I was back home in Shreveport. I
needed some help, and God was the place I knew I could get
it. I read my Bible and prayed, trying to get my head straight
and fight through the depression that I was living with constantly. I would come into my apartment, put on a Merle
Haggard tape, lie across the bed, and say, *Bradshaw, what is
wrong? Why can't you play football? What is wrong?* I worried myself sick.

That night after the Cincinnati game I hit rock bottom;
and for one day decided to give it all up and go into the
ministry. I was confused, and that was the direction I turned.
That week in practice the tension was so thick you could
bounce up against it. Noll was displeased with me and
showed it. The papers had some new tidbit every day, calling
Hanratty and me the "Babes in Toyland" quarterbacks, and
quoting me as saying that playing behind Hanratty would
"just ruin me" (which I didn't say). The papers were really
teeing off on me now. One writer pointed out that the year

before, Hanratty had been benched as a rookie QB in favor of Dick Shiner and had taken it graciously. Another writer quoted Hanratty as saying, "So many quarterbacks get impatient too quick, and when they're traded they don't blossom out." The writer added his own postscript: "It sounded like a message for someone."

13
End-of-Season Nightmare

FINALLY COACH NOLL told the sportswriters to cool it, that they were magnifying the problem, and putting undue pressure on both of us. Then he announced that Hanratty would be starting that Sunday against the New York Jets.

The Jets drew the biggest crowd of the year to Three Rivers Stadium, and we whipped them good. *They* whipped them good. I stood on the sidelines all afternoon with my helmet in my hand, and didn't get into the game for a single play. When I trotted out onto the field to warm up before the game, the crowd booed me, and that was the closest I came to being involved in the action. Joe Namath was out with an injury, and the Jets were having a bad year. We played well and beat them 21–17. That win put our season record at 4–4, and suddenly we were tied with the Cleveland Browns for the division lead.

Namath was in Pittsburgh with the team, and after the game the local sportswriters asked him for a comment on my statement that I wouldn't ride the bench behind Hanratty. He obliged them: "I'll tell you this, when you're under contract to a team, you do what they want you to do. If the coach wants you to play second-string behind a second-year man, that's what you do. The thing is, man, when you're playing behind a second-year man, it's nobody's fault but your own." And to go along with that quote, one of the photographers took a picture of me standing on the sidelines blowing a big bubble with some bubble gum I was chewing, and plastered that photo on the front page.

The policy seemed to be: WHEN YOU GET A GUY DOWN, KICK HIM!

The next week the Kansas City Chiefs came into town and beat us 31–14 behind a super passing performance by Lenny Dawson. If Hanratty had played well in that game I don't think I would ever have gotten in, but he had a tough time and by midway of the 3rd quarter we were down 17–0, so Noll gave me a chance to see what I could do.

When I came into the game, those crazy, fickle Pittsburgh fans had the audacity to applaud me! Can you believe it? One week they boo me when I warm up—the next week Hanratty has a bad day so they applaud when I replace him. Fickle? You'd better believe it! But I guess they're like football fans everywhere—they want a winner. I directed two TD drives and passed well. I had three interceptions, but all were on deflections, and Coach Noll seemed pleased with the job I did. So the see-saw tilted one more time: I was announced as the starting quarterback for the Cincinnati Bengal game the next week in Cincinnati.

It was Cincinnati's game all the way. They were coming on strong in the Central Division, and they beat us 34–7. I started in good fashion, but got bogged down after being clobbered on a late hit by Ernie Baccaglio. The Bengals got a 15-yard roughing-the-passer penalty out of it, but I got a badly bruised arm and wasn't worth a flip the rest of the day. Hanratty relieved me in the second half, following the alternating-quarterbacks plan.

Back home to face Cleveland, we won a big one that put us right back in the race for the division title. If ever a defensive unit won a game, our defense did that day. They were tough. They held the great running back Leroy Kelly to zero yards in ten carries; and held quarterback Bill Nelsen to 85 yards in passing. The defense scored on a 30-yard interception with 49 seconds to play in the first half. Andy Russell played like a madman, got a brain concussion in the 3rd quarter and didn't even come out of the game. When it was over, he didn't remember a thing that had happened since half time.

In the second half, it was my turn to play quarterback and I got off a couple of good ones. Ron Shanklin came up to me on the sidelines between offensive series and told me he thought he could beat Erich Barnes deep. I said okay. When we got the ball back we were on our own 19-yard line, but we tried the play anyway, and Shanklin beat him by three steps. I laid the ball right on him and he went for an 81-yard TD. On the very next offensive play following the Browns punt, Frenchy Fuqua got loose over the middle for another six points, this one a 57-yarder.

And suddenly we were in the driver's seat to win the

division championship. Our victory threw the Central Division race into a three-way tie, with us, Cleveland, and Cincinnati holding identical won-loss records of 5–6. We had three games to play, and they would be against the lowly Green Bay Packers (5 wins, 6 losses), the lowly Atlanta Falcons (3 wins, 7 losses, 1 tie), and the lowly Philadelphia Eagles (2 wins, 10 losses, 1 tie). All we had to do was win those three games. The mood around Pittsburgh changed, and enthusiasm was everywhere.

When we played Green Bay, it was cold as whiz, and we were behind almost before the fans had time to get into their seats. We lost the coin toss, kicked off to Green Bay, and Larry Krause ran the kickoff back 100 yards to put us behind 6–0. They missed the point after, and a few minutes later we narrowed the margin to 6–3 with a field goal. I came in to play quarterback in the second half. We started moving the ball well. Early in the 3rd quarter we got one of those big plays that so often turn a game around. With a first-and-ten on our 13-yard line, I dropped back into my end zone and turned the ball loose just before the pass rushers crashed me. The ball hit Dave Smith down the sidelines deep, and he took it all the way in for an 87-yard touchdown to put us ahead 9–6.

After that two things happened: we (meaning me) did everything wrong and they (meaning Bart Starr) did everything right. After that TD pass I couldn't get anything to work. We had talked it over in the locker room at half time and decided that we could beat Green Bay deep, so Noll's strategy was to throw the long bomb on them. On that first play it worked like a charm. But after that—nothing. The rest of the afternoon was an exercise in futility. Everything I threw up was batted down or intercepted, and I finished the day with a paltry 3 out of 20 and 4 interceptions. The defense caught more of my passes than the receivers did.

On the other side of the field, my old hero Bart Starr was conducting a course called "How to Dissect a Defense." He was super, and I stood on the sidelines watching him and thought about how many times I had seen him on TV as a kid, and how much more fun it was to worship the guy in the eighth grade than to play against him in Pittsburgh. He killed us.

The sportswriters didn't miss an opportunity to point out the contrast, of course. "The Steeler defeat," began the lead story the next morning, "was the difference between the 36-year-old Packer quarterback and Terry Bradshaw, the 22-year-old phenomenon who pitched the second half for the Steelers. Bradshaw, after hitting Smith with an 87-yard TD in the third quarter, appeared to forget football is a team game and was trying to do everything himself thereafter."

No comment.

Even though we had lost our advantage, we still weren't out of it. With wins over weak Atlanta and Philadelphia, and a loss by Cinncinnati, we could still tie for the championship. We got ready for Atlanta with that in mind. We *had* to win to stay in the race, and we all knew that we could do it. After such a lousy game against Green Bay, I knew that I wouldn't start, and might not even play.

I played, all right, and the way I played drove the last nail into my coffin. Hanratty played the entire first half, played it well, and probably should have stayed in the game. When the 3rd quarter opened, we were ahead 16–10, and Hanratty had moved the ball consistently in the first half. But Noll was committed to his two-quarterback system, and he really was determined to give me a chance to develop; he also thought that my passing game was tailor-made for the Falcons' defense. It was tailor-made for them, all right, just not to *score* against them. I came in at 16–10. On my first play in the game, I threw an interception from deep in our territory to give them a 17-yard field goal. So now it was 16–13, and there's more to come! After the kickoff, I rolled out to throw on the first play and threw the ball right into the face of John Zook, Atlanta's great defensive end. He was as surprised as I was, and clomped down inside our 5-yard line with the ball to set up an easy touchdown. That made it 16–20. They were ahead to stay and we were out of the Central Division race.

I spent most of that half lying flat on my back with Falcons on top of me—until Coach Noll finally pulled me out of the game and let Hanratty finish. When I came to the sidelines, he couldn't resist one shot: "I don't care how good you are, Terry. You can't play this game without studying it." I was hot and frustrated and mad and bruised and came close to telling him some things that rookies just don't say to their coaches. But I did the only smart thing I had done all day. I sat down on the bench without saying a word.

By this time it's no-holds-barred on the sports pages, and

the Pittsburgh writers couldn't wait to get to their typewriters to tell the world how bad I was. "Bradshaw came into the game and promptly passed the Steelers into chaos," one wrote. Another was more descriptive: "Bradshaw looked bad. He had no control of himself, galloped along behind the line of scrimmage and unleashed the ball with no idea where it was going."

This constant barrage of criticism from the press turned the honeymoon that I had enjoyed with the Pittsburgh public in the early season into a nightmare. People would come up to me right on the street and ask me why I was letting the Steelers down, and why I said all those terrible things I said. Eventually I quit going out at all. One of the few people I saw was my friend and Pittsburgh attorney, Les Zittrain. I stayed in my apartment or at the stadium practically all the time.

And letters! Did I ever get letters! Here is a small sample:

Dear Mr. Bradshaw:

    You are undoubtedly the worst quarterback I have ever seen. . . .

Dear Mr. Bradshaw:

    What a waste for the Steelers to spend their best draft choice on you. . . .

Dear Mr. Bradshaw:

    How can you live with yourself, ruining Mr. Rooney's team the way you have . . . ?

Dear Mr. Bradshaw:
    I am so sick of watching you and the Steelers lose that it makes me vomit. . . .

Dear Mr. Bradshaw:
    You stink. . . .

Dear Mr. Bradshaw:
    My husband and I watch you on TV, and we think you are degenerate. . . .

The nightmare started to get to me. I knew these people —writers, fans, coaches, everybody—were disappointed, but what did they want me to do? I was trying as hard as I possibly could. I wanted to play good ball more than anybody, but it just wasn't working out that way. What did they think—that I was throwing those interceptions on purpose? that I was losing because I was mean? or because I hated Pittsburgh? The pressure was about to put me under, and the more I worried, the worse I played. By December I was just hanging on by my fingernails, hoping the season would hurry up and end so I could go home and lick my wounds. The Pittsburgh fans are the greatest, but at that point I was convinced everybody had it in for me.

    The last game of the season was against the Philadelphia Eagles, and we should have beaten them like a drum. After that Atlanta game even Chuck Noll gave up on me, and I didn't play quarterback at all in the game. By this time I didn't even care. I had given up. I stood on the sidelines with absolutely no interest in the game whatsoever. Bobby Walden, our punter, had been hurt and I was called on to punt (since I had done some punting in college and could kick the ball fairly well).

The first punting situation came, and I went in to do my job. When the snap came back to me, one of their defensive linemen came roaring through the line without being touched. He blocked the ball just as it left my foot, and came flying right on into me. He almost tore my leg off, and Mike Dirks fell on the ball in the Steeler end zone for a touchdown. The second time I came in to punt, I was so spooked by having the first one blocked that I could think of nothing but getting the ball away in a hurry. I'll bet that was the quickest punt in NFL history. By the time that ball hit my hands— *Boom!*—it was gone. I had the punt away in a hurry, all right, for a whopping distance of 17 yards! So much for my career as a pro punter. We lost the game 30–20 to end the season in third place in the Central Division of the American Football Conference with a record of five wins and nine losses. That was a long way up from 1–13, but it was a disappointing season after all the hopes that had been raised in the fall. And probably that was the heart of the problem my rookie year—expectations that were too high to be met. In the first place, I had expected too much of myself. Things had seemed so simple during those last two years at Tech, and I came to pro football with the feeling that I could just start there where I ended in college. The early success in preseason games reinforced that illusion, and when the hard reality—that becoming a seasoned NFL quarterback takes a while—sank in, the public was more disgusted than ever.

In addition to the problem of unrealistic expectations, the main source of my trouble that rookie year was simply my own immaturity. I didn't know how to cope with defeat—with what I considered to be a hostile press—with the pressure of living my life in a fishbowl. I went to Pittsburgh with a lot of growing up to do, and unfortunately I had to do most of it under conditions that were perfect for getting a talkative, uninhibited person like me into trouble. At any rate, when the gun sounded to end the final game against Philadelphia, I had only one thought in mind—to get out of Pittsburgh as soon as possible. I hated everybody in the world, and—as far as I could tell—everybody in the world hated me.

Six hours after our team charter landed in Pittsburgh, I had cleaned out my apartment and was back at the airport leaving for home. To show you how jinxed I was, I boarded a plane bound for Shreveport; it developed trouble in its hydraulic system, and we had to make a crash landing on the runway at the Chicago airport! That incident seemed the most appropriate conclusion I can imagine to my rookie year. It reminded me of something that Hank Williams, the great country singer, used to say: "Don't worry about anything—nothing's gonna work out right anyhow."

14
Growing Up—At Last

AFTER A FEW WEEKS' rest back in Shreveport, I returned to school at Louisiana Tech to complete the final quarter of work that I needed for my degree. That two-month stretch at Tech was good for me. One thing about a college campus —people who want to be left alone are usually left alone, and that's exactly what I wanted. Occasionally, people would spot me and say, "Hey, aren't you Terry Bradshaw?" and if they were inclined to believe I wasn't, that was all right with me. I didn't want to talk about the Steelers; I wanted a few months to drain my brain of every thought of football.

At first I tried not to think about the future. I didn't want to think about what I was going to do the next year. My immediate impulse was to quit, but as the trauma of the rookie season got farther into the past, I realized that it would be impossible for me to do that. I had never been a quitter, and I couldn't start quitting now. The worst of it had to be behind me, I figured, so why not go back the next year and prove to myself and the Steelers and the Pittsburgh fans and the NFL that I *could* do the job. I realized that I had given up during my rookie year, and everybody expected me to just fade off the scene. I decided to show them I could be the best. And when I made up my mind to do that, I started looking forward to my second year.

When training camp opened the next July, I was eager to get there. I couldn't wait to see the "depth chart"—the list of players released by the team at the beginning of camp which shows the players at each position in order of their expected use. For the last few weeks before camp started I wondered who would be at the top of that chart in the quarterback spot, Hanratty or me? I got to camp and could hardly believe it when I saw my name at the top of the list. That thrilled me like nothing had in months. It was a vote of confidence from the coaching staff that I really needed to get me going, and it made me doubly determined to win back the respect of my teammates that I had in preseason the year before.

I had a good training camp, and played well in the preseason games. I threw the ball well, and gradually began to feel the rhythm that goes along with good quarterbacking. My attitude was 100 percent improved. In the year before my confidence had been totally demolished, and now I could feel it building up again. I concentrated on getting up every day with my mind on exactly how I wanted to call signals, set up to throw, release the ball, and all the little things that a quarterback does out on the field.

There was a coaching change made before that second training camp that made an enormous difference in my play. The Steelers hired Babe Parilli as a special coach for the quarterbacks. Parilli had been a great signal-caller himself. He was an All-American at the University of Kentucky, then went on to play sixteen years of pro ball. He was one of the early heroes of the American Football League, winning the Most-Valuable-Player award in that league in 1964. When Parilli came to the Steelers it gave me someone to lean on for the first time since I had become a pro. We became good friends, and he became someone I could talk to, confide in, and share personal things with. When I had something on my chest, I could talk to Babe about it and get it out in the open, instead of bottling it up inside. That made an enormous difference in my morale and my attitude—and consequently in my play on the field.

We lost only one game in the preseason that year. The quarterback situation seemed to stabilize with me as the starter and Hanratty number two. Toward the end of the preseason I began to worry about choking when play started for keeps. We opened against Chicago and I got uptight, threw four interceptions. We lost. Warren Bankston fumbled late in the game and it cost us the TD that was the margin of defeat. Bankston and I stood in the shower after the game and cried because we had wanted to win that first one so badly. The game was a classic example of how a team can lose by interceptions and fumbles. We outgained the Bears 352 yards to 141, and they beat us. The reason: we lost the ball 7 times to their 1 on fumbles and intercepted passes.

The fear that gnawed at me in the shower that day was that this season was going to follow the same pattern as the last one—a great preseason, then everything goes down the drain when it starts counting.

It wasn't the same, though. We came right back to beat the Bengals and the San Diego Chargers at home the next two weeks. Our defense, now beginning to jell, saved us from losing—and me from being the goat—with a great goal-line stand. We were ahead 21–17, and had the ball with time running out on the clock. All I had to do was fall on the ball for three plays and it was all over. But I thought I saw a hole and tried to run through it for extra yardage—and fumbled. That set them up inside our ten-yard line, and a touchdown would win for them. I stood on the sidelines and pulled for those guys on defense for all I was worth—and they stopped the Chargers cold to save the victory. I wanted to buy them all dinner that night; but the way those guys eat, I didn't have the money!

Then we lost a couple of games on the road—to the Browns in the mud at Cleveland and to the Kansas City Chiefs on Monday night TV. After looking so bad the year before on Monday night television, I really got psyched up for the Kansas City game. When the kickoff came it was pouring rain, and it rained all through the contest. It's hard to maintain your intensity for long in a pouring rain. I had a good passing game (20 of 39 for 269 yards), but not good enough, and we lost it.

Back home, we rebounded by beating Houston to even our season record at 3–3. Early in the season Coach Noll did something that did wonders for my self-confidence. He told me that I was the team's quarterback. Period. "Don't worry if you have a bad game," he said. "You're the quarterback and you're going to play. I don't intend to pull you just because you have a bad game. So just relax and play the kind of ball you're capable of." What a difference that made to me! I settled down, quit worrying about somebody getting my job, and started to throw the ball well for the first time since my college days.

Against Houston we almost cost ourselves the game by costly penalties. We had 113 yards in penalties that day. In one stretch we drove from *our* 20-yard line-to *their* 3-yard line, got four straight penalties that pushed us all the way back past midfield, then drove back down inside the ten, had another penalty back to the twenty-five, and ended up settling for a field goal. You can't win ball games that way. I hit 21 of 32 passes, and it was barely enough.

After a loss on the road to Baltimore, we came back home to beat the Cleveland Browns. In that Cleveland game I twisted my ankle trying to pull out of the grasp of a tackler. I hobbled over to the sidelines with pain shooting up my leg, afraid the ankle was broken and I would be out for the year. I left the stadium immediately to go to Divine Providence Hospital for X rays, and listened on the radio while Terry Hanratty came in to do a super job and maintain our lead. The ankle wasn't broken, so by the middle of the week I was working out for the game against the Miami Dolphins.

We had heard so much about the Dolphins that we were psyched sky-high by the time the game started. We got the ball, marched right down the field, and scored. We got the ball again, moved down the field and scored again. Then a third time we got the ball and scored. *Bang! Bang! Bang!* Three touchdown passes the first three possessions, and we had a 21-3 lead. After that it was all Miami. They got one TD back on us, then another, and finally beat us 24-21 on a 60-yard bomb late in the final quarter. It was a sickening way to lose a ball game, especially against a team that was being touted as highly as the Dolphins.

Back home we beat the New York Giants 17-13. It was cold and snowy for the game. Fran Tarkenton gave our defense headaches all day, and rolled up a ton of yardage against us, but could only punch the ball over the goal line once—and that wasn't enough to beat us.

We dropped the next two games and I'll never know why. Those games cost us a winning season, and on both occasions we should have won. Somehow we just weren't ready for the games mentally. We were flat, and too many guys had "down" days at the same time. Denver and Houston beat us. We were better than both those teams, but they beat us soundly. Against Denver I was pulled from the game in hopes that Hanratty could generate some offense. It's amazing what a difference a year makes. A year before I was demolished every time I played poorly and was pulled for Hanratty. This time I was unhappy, naturally, but it didn't wipe me out. I was secure as the #1 quarterback, and was able to shrug it off as a bad day, realize that those will come occasionally, and go on. That's what they call maturity—and that's what I *didn't* have the year before.

Against Cincinnati the next week I had been sick and

didn't start. Coach Noll told me during the week that I was "physically and emotionally drained," and that he would try to keep me out of the game altogether if he could. We fell behind in the third quarter, and he called on me. I came in and threw 2 touchdown passes, and we won the game 21–13. It was one of the most satisfying days of my career—to be able to come through in the clutch when I was needed.

The season ended the next Sunday against the Los Angeles Rams, and we wanted the victory to give us a break-even season at seven wins and seven losses. It was not to be. We lost the game 23–14, finishing the year with a 6–8 record.

The Steelers didn't win the divisional title that year, and we certainly didn't establish ourselves as one of the power-houses of the National Football League, but it was a good, solid year nevertheless, and when I packed my bags for Shreveport after the season, I felt that I had proven myself as an NFL quarterback, and was on the way to achieving some of the goals I had set for myself in pro ball. The Steelers had made an apparently small improvement in their record (5–9 to 6–8), but all of us on the team sensed that we were much closer to becoming a championship-calibre team than that small change indicated.

As far as my personal performance was concerned, the difference between year one and year two was like the difference between daylight and dark. To begin with, I had established myself as the starting quarterback and the leader of the offensive unit.

I had also improved as a passer. Compare these statistics:

completion percentage, 37 percent as a rookie, 54 percent in my second year; touchdown passes 6 as a rookie, 13 in my second year; total yards passing, 1410 as a rookie, 2259 my second year. My rookie season I led the NFL in interceptions, and I cut down on those my second year. And I was the top running quarterback in the conference my second year, where as a rookie, I hadn't even come close.

15
Missy

THERE WERE LOTS of reasons for the change from 1970 to 1971, most of which I have already mentioned. But perhaps the biggest reason is one that didn't appear on the stat sheets or the sports pages. The biggest reason was a person—someone who came along during that second year and made the whole game more meaningful and all my goals more important to me. Football may be a physical game, but the influence of those off-the-field emotions is enormous.

Her name was Melissa Babish. She had big brown eyes and a beautiful smile, and when I first met her I was lying on my back in a hospital bed in Pittsburgh. It was the spring after I had been drafted, and I was at Divine Providence Hospital recovering from the surgery to remove a calcium deposit on my thigh. How she got there is one of those long, roundabout stories that go well in soap operas and romance magazines.

It was one of those deals where I knew someone who knew her, and when I had to enter the hospital in Pittsburgh, my friend called her and suggested she come by to visit me. *Okay,* she thought, *Why not? Maybe it will cheer him up.* So here I was, lying in the hospital feeling sorry for myself because I was away from home with nobody around who knew me, when all of a sudden there stood this beautiful girl in the doorway, come to visit me.

That's how we met, and as soon as I was able to get up and move around, I called to ask for a date. I remember that on that first date we went to see the Pirates play baseball with Missy driving and me still on crutches. We dated a few times during my rookie year, and I called her occasionally, but throughout that season our relationship was a hit-or-miss thing. She was a University of Pittsburgh student, majoring in psychology, and far removed from the world of the Steelers, so our paths rarely crossed.

Missy was a native of Pittsburgh. I saw very quickly that she was different from the typical, star-struck teen-ager. She just wasn't bowled over by the grand and glorious glamour of going out with the great Terry Bradshaw, professional quarterback, and there was a reason. When I met her, Missy had just completed a year's reign as Miss Teenage America. She had been down the "celebrity" route herself, and the experience had given her a bearing and poise and sense of style that most eighteen-year-olds don't have. She was a classy gal, and even though we saw little of each other that rookie year, I always kept in touch.

The experience as Miss Teenage America had not been an entirely happy one for Missy. She entered the Miss Teenage Pittsburgh pageant at the urging of her cheerleaders' supervisor at South Fayette High School, where she was a senior. She won that contest and went to the national finals in Fort

Worth, Texas. That week of the finals was an unbroken delight, and when she was crowned Miss Teenage America in the nationally-televised pageant at the end of the week, it seemed like an All-American dream come true.

The dream became a nightmare. When she won, Missy became the property of the pageant's promoters, and before she even had time to go home to change her suitcase, she was sent on the road for a string of personal appearances in Chicago. The day she left Fort Worth, she began to feel more like a commodity than a queen. She was pushed and shoved from one appointment to another with little regard for her own feelings or convenience, given backbreaking schedules that kept her bone-tired most of the time, and generally felt exploited by the pageant organizers. She learned to put on a plastic smile in public, and give the same sweet answers to the endless interviews. Mostly she cried in her hotel room at night and grimly hung on for the duration. By the time she relinquished her crown to the next Miss Teenage America, she had already learned what I was going to learn as a rookie —that the glamorous public life of a "star" is often accompanied by a great deal of unhappiness and personal anguish in private.

When I returned to Pittsburgh for an off-season meeting after my rookie season, I was ready for the stable, no-nonsense approach that Missy had always taken toward the publicity surrounding me. She had paid little attention to the newspaper reports of how great I was in the first place, so she likewise ignored the bad stuff they said when things went sour. She wasn't awed by the fact that I was a pro-football player, since she had spent her time in the spotlight, too. So she was able to do something which none of the other girls whom I dated had done: She was able to see me for what I really was—a lonesome, discouraged, confused kid—and not some kind of carefree, footloose athlete.

It's not easy for a public figure to have a normal courtship. Getting a date is easy enough, but deciding who is interested in you for your own sake and who is interested in the attention that goes along with it is often a difficult job. With Missy there was never any doubt. I always knew that any attraction she felt for me had to be genuine. Corny as it sounds, I discovered that she was probably the only person in Pittsburgh who understood me and cared for me whether I was up or down.

Throughout my second year we dated regularly, and that relationship brought some stability into my personal life for the first time since I left Louisiana. She became a Steelers' fan, and knowing she was in the stands—or watching on TV —really gave me a lift and a new motivation that I hadn't had before. After the season was over, I left Pittsburgh and drove back south. About two weeks after I got home, it occurred to me that we were in love, we were good for one another, and it was time to get married. When Missy came down to spend New Year's with my folks, we decided to get married in April, and she went back to get ready for the wedding.

Within a week we had decided to move the date up to late

February, and within another week even that seemed too far away. About the end of January I decided that to wait any longer was unnecessary agony, so I called Missy, told her I was coming to Pittsburgh for a speaking engagement in ten days, and said I wanted to get married then. I could hear her *gulp* over the phone, saying she'd consider it and call me back. She didn't consider it long. She woke me up at 2:00 A.M. to tell me she thought the idea was a good one. "If God wants us to get married, it'll work out," she said.

The wedding went smoothly, considering that we had to change the site four times to keep the television and radio stations from giving out the location over the air! We had a small, private ceremony in a little chapel outside of Pittsburgh on February 11, 1972 *and* (knock on wood) lived happily ever after.

16
That Championship Season

DURING THE 1972 season—my third in the NFL—I discovered all over again just how much fun football can be. No matter how many times it is said, it's still true—*nothing* can take the place of winning. Not setting records, not getting headlines, not making a lot of money—nothing beats winning. And in 1972, the Pittsburgh Steelers finally broke through to the super year that owner Art Rooney and the Pittsburgh fans had dreamed of for so long. We went 11–3, won the championship of the Central Division of the AFC, and went to the second round of the playoffs before losing to the Super Bowl Champs, the Miami Dolphins.

From the very start of the training camp things looked good for us. We finally had the cast of characters that could win a championship. Once again Coach Noll had come up with a good year in the draft. The prize, of course, was Franco Harris, the Penn State running back who was Pittsburgh's first choice. The year before, we had depended too heavily on the passing game, and Noll went into the draft with the idea of getting more firepower for that part of our offense. He got a good one. I remember watching Franco work out early in training camp and being unimpressed. He didn't look bad, but there was certainly nothing about him that would have set him apart from dozens of other backs around the country. I began to wonder if maybe the coaches had missed in going for him in the first round. But when the preseason games started, and Franco got turned loose in the field, he was a different guy altogether. He ran with such an awesome combination of power and speed and quickness that I could hardly believe he was the same Franco Harris I had seen in training camp. I knew then that the Steelers had a real jewel, and by the end of the year every football fan in the country knew it.

Another good rookie was tight end John McMakin, from Clemson. He is big and strong (6'3", 225 pounds), and has tremendous desire to make it as a top NFL tight end. Our wide receivers, Ron Shanklin and Frank Lewis, are, in my opinion, as good as any pair of receivers in the league. I absolutely wouldn't trade them for any other two receivers anywhere.

And there is another group on our team that I believe is the best in the league. That is the offensive line. Believe me, a quarterback lives or dies by the skill of his offensive line. Without good play from the lineman in front of him, he eats dirt all day—no matter how gifted he is. Our front line is young and tough. When they are right, they can blow a hole in the defense big enough to drive a cement truck through. Ray Mansfield, our veteran center, was especially helpful to me in the early years when I was just beginning to learn NFL defenses. The younger guys—like Jon Kolb, Bruce Van Dyke, Gerry Mullins, Sam Davis, and Jim Clack—provide the muscle that makes our offense go.

Added to those guys were the defense which had already become a respected squad the year before. They were led by Joe Greene. Joe is one of the nicest, gentlest, warmest human beings I've ever met, but when you put him in a Steeler uniform and line him up on the field across from a quarterback in a different uniform, he'd kill his grandmother to get to him. Along with him there is Andy Russell, an All-Pro linebacker whose experience helps stabilize the defense, and Jack Ham, another Penn State product who as a second-year linebacker became one of the best young defensive players in the game.

And perhaps most importantly, we had the best head coach in the league. He knows how to draft; he knows how to keep his team "up" for an entire season; and he can find that certain two or three plays that will beat the other team's defense in any given game. Not only that, but he is a coach in the true sense of the word—not only a strategist or an on-the-field administrator—but a *coach*. He doesn't just tell his players what to do—he teaches them how to do it.

We started the preseason by scoring over fifty points against the New Orleans Saints, and it seemed like there was a storm building up in Pittsburgh. Everyone could sense that something was going to happen. It was just *different*—almost like we knew that we were on the verge of a great year.

Our last preseason game was against the Washington Redskins. They were tough as nails, and we knew if we could beat them we could beat everybody. We treated that game almost like a season opener—that's how seriously we took it. We felt this would tell us what kind of team we had. We started our regulars and they started theirs, and the game ended in a 10–10 tie. After that we knew we were ready to play ball.

We opened against Oakland, and we needed that game to prove to ourselves that we could beat a top dog. For the last two years we had beat the easy teams, but now it was time for us to start beating the tough ones, and we took it to them. It took a 4th quarter surge by Lamonica to keep it from being a stomp. We beat them soundly, and when it was over we weren't surprised. It was good to break the opening-day jinx, especially after the two lousy openers I had suffered through in other years.

We went on the road to Cincinnati and lost. We took the lead at half time, but couldn't hold it for two more quarters. But for some reason that loss didn't get the team down. We came out of the game knowing we should have won it, and that we would get another shot at them back home in Pittsburgh later in the year. The loss slowed our momentum a little, but it really didn't take the edge off our confidence.

One thing that loss did for us was make us eager to get the St. Louis Cardinals the next week. We had a great week of practice, and wanted to show that we could win on the road. Traditionally, the Steelers have played well at home and poorly on the road. The year before, we had been 5–5 after our first ten games—5 victories at home and 5 losses on the road. A team obviously can't win a championship that way. We had to start winning on the road, and we figured this was the time. Well, when the game started, we were worldbeaters from 5–yard line to 5–yard line, but we couldn't score. And when you don't score, you don't win.

With 1:26 left in the game, we were down by 6 points, and had to have a last-minute, 70-yard drive if we were going to pull the game out of the fire. I hit a couple of passes, and we pushed well into their territory. I called time-out and went to the sidelines. Chuck Noll set up a play to use if they put a certain defense on us—a pass to wide receiver Frank Lewis. "Just lay the ball out and let Lewis run under it," he said. When I came to the line of scrimmage, they shifted into that defense, Lewis found the open spot, I laid the ball out there to him and he ran right under it for a TD with less than half a minute left. We won the game 25–19. So we not only showed ourselves we could win on the road, but that we could come from behind to do it!

The press coverage of that game convinced me of something I've always suspected: Sportswriters are nothing but a bunch of quarterbacks at heart. When you pass, they want you to run; when you run, they want you to pass. There's no way to please all of them. Even when you win, if they don't like the *way* you win, they get onto you. I had thrown 40 passes in the St. Louis game (completed 25 of them), and one of the local columnists thought that was too many. So we won the game and he wants to fuss about *how* we won it. There was a difference, though, from this criticism and that of my rookie year—this criticism I didn't pay any attention to. I figured, *If I'm passing too much, Coach Noll will tell me, and so I won't worry about it.*

We played in Dallas the next week, and the whole day was a Bad Day at Black Rock. The Cowboys' defense was super-tough, but so was ours. At half time we took a 13–10 lead into the dressing room, but soon after intermission they scored on a 55–yard bomb to Ron Sellers thrown by—get this—half-back Calvin Hill. That put us behind 17–13, and we just couldn't seem to penetrate their defense after that. Finally, in the closing seconds, we started another drive. We started on our 20 with less than 2 minutes left, and ground the ball all the way down to their 20, first-and-ten with only a few seconds remaining and all our time-outs gone. I threw three straight incompletions, the last one stopping the clock with one second left in the game. I scrambled with time gone on that last play, found Frank Lewis in the end zone, and threw the ball right between his arms. It wasn't Frank's fault—the sun was shining right in his eyes through that stupid hole in the roof of the stadium, and completely blinded him. But we lost the game, and had nothing to show for all the bruises we took back to Pittsburgh with us.

The next week our defense played a great game, and we beat the Houston Oilers. That was the first game in which we really ran the ball, and the devastating running attack that came to dominate our offense began to emerge that afternoon. The New England Patriots came in the next week and we just blew them right out of the stadium. The final score was 33–3; I threw only 11 passes all afternoon and just sat back and let the running backs eat them up. The victory put us 4–2 for the year, and moved us into a tie with Cincinnati for the division lead.

We traveled to Buffalo the next Sunday and beat the Bills, with Franco Harris erupting for another great running performance. But a rumor that got started before the game (and circulated until after it was over) came close to ruining the whole occasion for me that day. The rumor had to do with my father. Someone called the Buffalo press box about half an hour before the kickoff to report that my father had just been killed in an automobile accident in Louisiana that afternoon.

I had already showered and dressed after the game, and was sitting on the team bus waiting for the drive to the airport, when a Pittsburgh reporter came running onto the bus and asked me if I had heard about my father being killed. "Man, what are you talking about?" I asked. I thought I had heard him wrong.

"We got a phone call in the press box saying that your dad was killed in a car wreck today," he responded.

I took off. I ran off that bus, past the fans that were still hanging around, back into the stadium, and sprinted to the nearest phone I could find. I had noticed everyone acting strange around me in the locker room after the game, and now it made sense why: They had heard the news before I did.

I dialed my folks' number in Shreveport, and the line was

busy. That did it. I could visualize the crowd of people there at the house with my mother, and someone on the phone calling relatives and making arrangements. I panicked. I got the operator on the phone and asked her to break in on the busy line at the house. When she called, the phone was clear, and my little brother Craig answered.

"Craig?" I asked. There was nothing but a muffled *hello* on the other end.

"Craig, is Dad there?" This time I was shouting into the receiver. Still no answer.

Then Dad's voice came on the line, *"Hello!"* loud and booming and healthy.

I just burst out crying, and bawled like a baby until finally my mom came on the phone to talk to me. I told her what had happened, and she started crying, too, and we all three had a time telling each other we loved one another.

I believe some bookies started that rumor, hoping the word would get to me sooner and upset me before the game started. And they almost succeeded. If the message had reached me before I took the field, I wouldn't have been worth shooting in the ball game. As it was, I was badly frightened, and was still shook up when I got home that night. I called my Dad again when I got home, in fact, to make sure I hadn't made a mistake!

We were tied for the division lead with the Bengals, and our next game was against them in Pittsburgh. This was a *must* game for us—not that we needed any special motivation to get ready for the Bengals. There are some teams you just like to beat more than others, and I believe I'd rather beat Cincinnati than anybody. I don't know why, but lots of guys on our team feel the same way. They are obvious rivals —young like us, in the same division, located just over the state line in Ohio. One of the few cheap shots that I've ever taken in the NFL came from Bill Bergey of the Bengals, and I've enjoyed beating them even more since then.

We beat the Bengals like a drum that day. I had my best passing day of the season, throwing 3 TD passes. Frank Lewis, our young receiver, had a great day catching the ball. One thing I remember well is that Mike Reid, their defensive lineman, spouted off a lot during the game. Normally there is very little talk back and forth between teams on the field, but on this particular day Reid fussed and cried and cussed all day long. We ran the ball at him all day, and he didn't like it very much, I guess. The only thing I know to do when a defensive lineman jaws at me is to run about an 80–yard drive right down his throat, and that's what we did to Reid that day.

The Kansas City Chiefs came into town the next week, and all week long in practice Coach Noll told us that we could beat them. I was really afraid of being smeared by the Chiefs, and I guess it showed, because Noll kept hammering home to me the idea that we could beat them. And he was right. We were going so good now that we were all playing as a unit, and the fans were loving it. Once those Pittsburgh fans decided we were for real, they became the best fans in the league. Franco Harris had his own private rooting section spring up, calling themselves Franco's Italian Army. Placekicker Roy Gerela's fans called themselves Gerela's Gorillas, sat in the end-zone bleachers, and one of them started coming to the home games dressed in a gorilla costume. The enthusiasm ran so high that it became difficult to go out into the public anytime at all without being practically mobbed. It was really wild! After forty years of frustration these fans finally had a winner, and they were eating it up. And so were we.

Cleveland slowed us down the next week behind a big game by quarterback Mike Phipps. It was the old familiar story—losing on the road to our divisional rivals. After the game Coach Noll laid the whip to us for the only time all year. He really jacked us up after that loss, reminded us of what all we had at stake, and we got the bit between our teeth again. We didn't lose another game the rest of the regular season. First we knocked off the Minnesota Vikings, then got a second crack at the Browns when they came in, and beat them. Then we went to Houston and squeaked past on a close, 9–7 ball game that clinched us a spot in the playoffs —the first time a Pittsburgh team had ever been there. In that game I suffered a dislocated finger on my throwing hand. I was throwing a pass, and on the follow-through jammed my finger into Elvin Bethea's face mask. That was the most painful injury I've ever had in football. It felt like having a finger slammed in a car door, and the joint came completely out of the socket. The trainer popped it back in on the sidelines, but I was out for the day, and rookie quarterback Joe Gilliam came in and did a fine job for the rest of the game.

We finished the season against San Diego on the coast— a game we had to win to nail down the division championship. We didn't want to back into the playoffs, and we took the game to the Chargers from the very first and beat them going away.

Then came the playoffs—the mass hysteria of the Pittsburgh fans, the miraculous, last-minute victory over the Oakland Raiders, and finally the end of the road against the Miami Dolphins.

17
No Easy Game

IT IS INCREASINGLY popular to knock the game of football these days.

You've probably heard the criticism more than once: that the game is too violent, that it is dehumanizing, that there are too many injuries. The biggest complaint of all is that football is just a game, and that any game is too trifling and unimportant to occupy such a prominent place in the lives of those who play it. And it is that last criticism that deserves an answer.

Football *is* a game, but it's no easy game. It is not simply twenty-two men butting heads together on a 100-yard field. It is a highly complex, physically-punishing game that requires of its players an extraordinary amount of physical and mental intensity. It is a tough, demanding game, and that is exactly where its value lies. Football doesn't necessarily build character, as the cliche says, but it does give a boy or a young man a setting in which he can learn to cope with life, learn to struggle and come out on top—learn that he can be a winner.

And once a fellow has learned that he is a winner, he's on

the way! He can take that knowledge and transfer it to any other part of his life. The big problem is to learn it—to learn that he can win, he can get up off the floor and come back, he can beat the odds and come out on top. And he can learn that about himself on the football field as well as anywhere in the world.

It is from its very difficulty that football derives its ability to affect lives with the impact that it does. I'll never forget how things changed on the Steelers when it finally dawned on us in that 1972 season that we were winners. We had players doing things they didn't know they could do—guys breaking tackles they didn't know they could break, catching passes they didn't know they could catch, running and blocking when we've never seen them run and block like that before.

We started going out the next week *feeling* we're going to win, *knowing* we're going to win. We were starting to do things as a team that we'd never done before.

And that is exactly what happened to me in my personal life—after I had come through that bad year as a rookie—and finally saw things start to fall in place for me. I began to cope with things I hadn't been able to cope with before, started handling problems I couldn't handle before, developed a kind of maturity I hadn't had before. I became a winner—a real-life winner. I knew I could do what had to be done, and I learned that on the football field.

Everyone has his own battles to fight, but for me, I've learned that living the life of a Christian is no easy game either. Being a committed Christian is the hardest thing in the world to do. It's much harder than being first team, making All-American, starting as a pro quarterback. But it is a pursuit that you can win at, too. Not by beating the next guy at it, or by making some kind of super accomplishment in the church, but simply by sticking with it—keeping God in your life—all the way through.

It takes a real tough individual to win at either game. I've had my share of winning and losing at both, and I know that staying on top—in football or in life—is no easy game.